TOP▷REQUEST

Classic Rock SHEET MUSIC

20 ALL-TIME FAVORITES ARRANGED BY DAN COATES

Contents

Produced by
Alfred Music
P.O. Box 10003
Van Nuys, CA 91410-0003
alfred.com

Produced in USA.

ISBN-10: 0-7390-9843-8
ISBN-13: 978-0-7390-9843-1

ANY WAY YOU WANT IT

Words and Music by
Neal Schon and Steve Perry
Arranged by Dan Coates

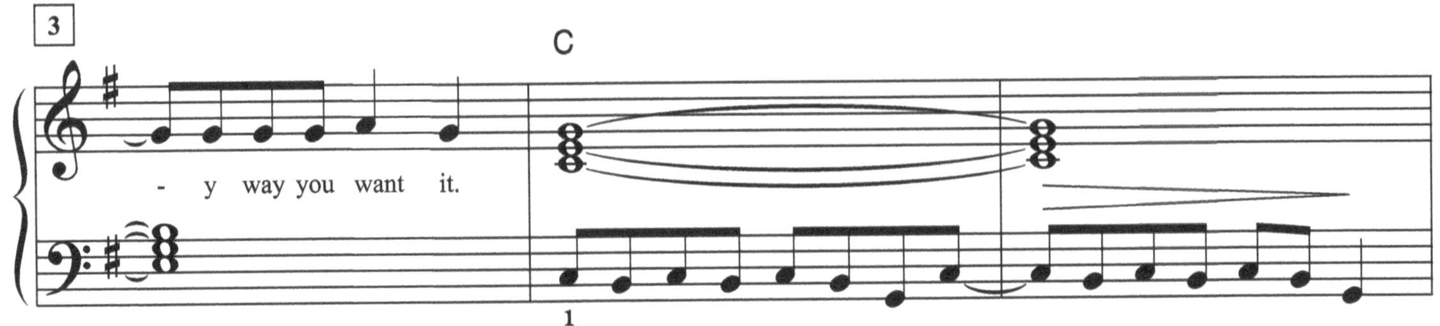

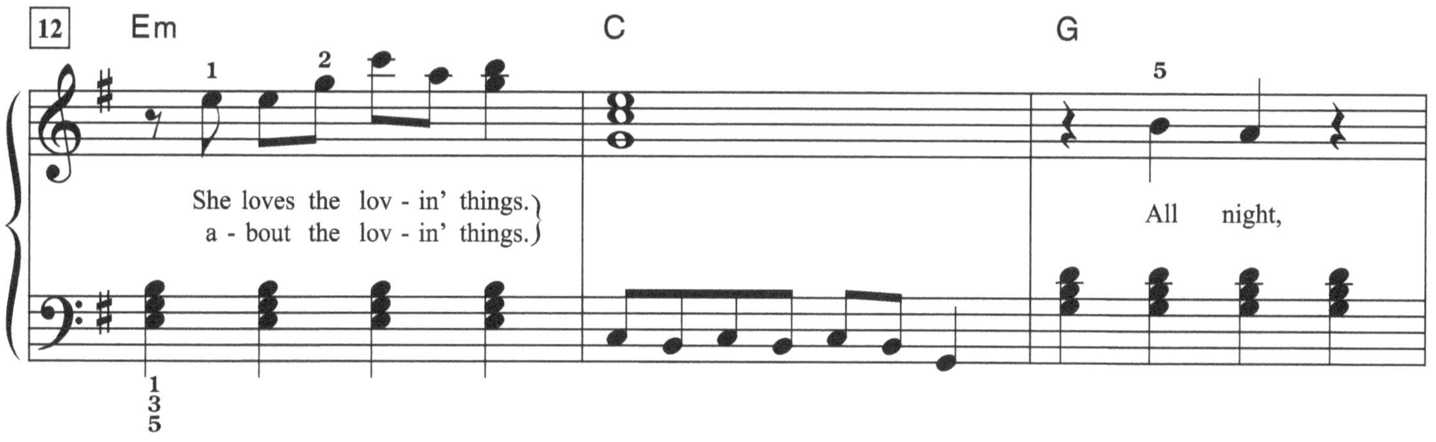
12
Em
C
G
1
2
5
She loves the lov - in' things.
a - bout the lov - in' things.
All night,
1
3
5

15
D/F♯
Em
C
all night,
oh, ev - 'ry night.

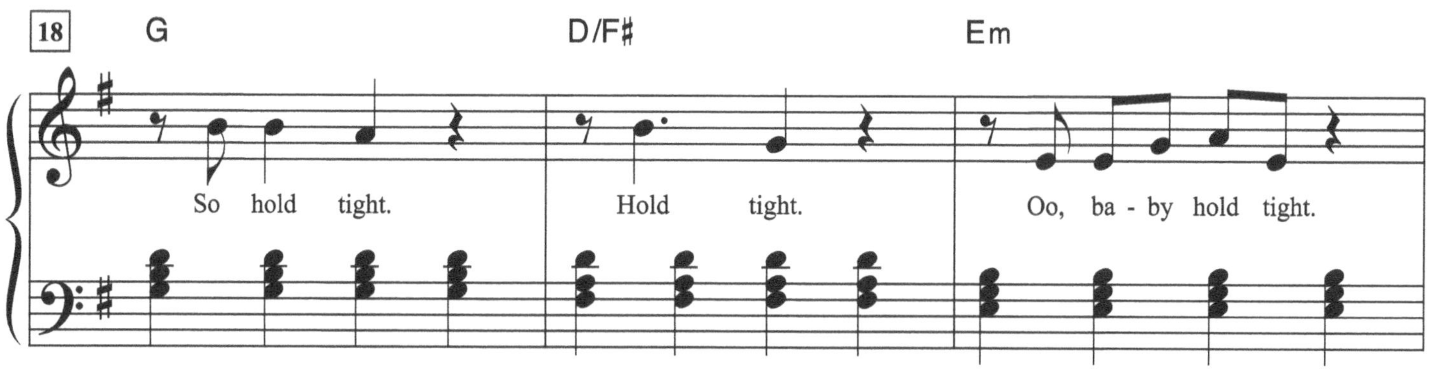
18
G
D/F♯
Em
So hold tight.
Hold tight.
Oo, ba - by hold tight.

Chorus:

21
C
G
D/F♯
1 2 3
She said, "An - y way you want it. That's the way you need it. An -
f

24
Em
C
G
3
y way you want it."
She said, "An
- y way you want it. That's
1
3
5

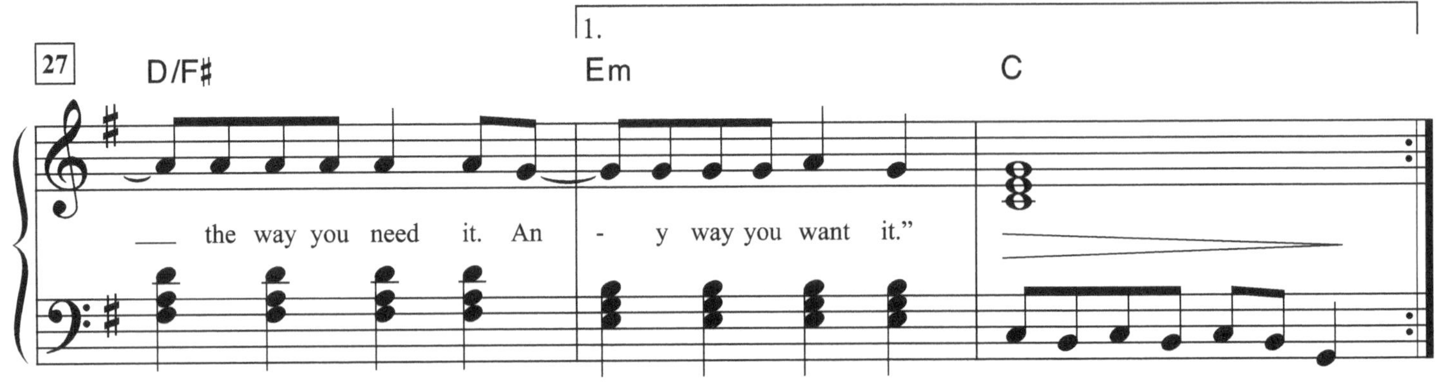
1.
27
D/F♯
Em
C
the way you need it. An
- y way you want it."

2.
30
Em
C
G
1 2 3
- y way you want it."
She said, "An
- y way you want it. That's

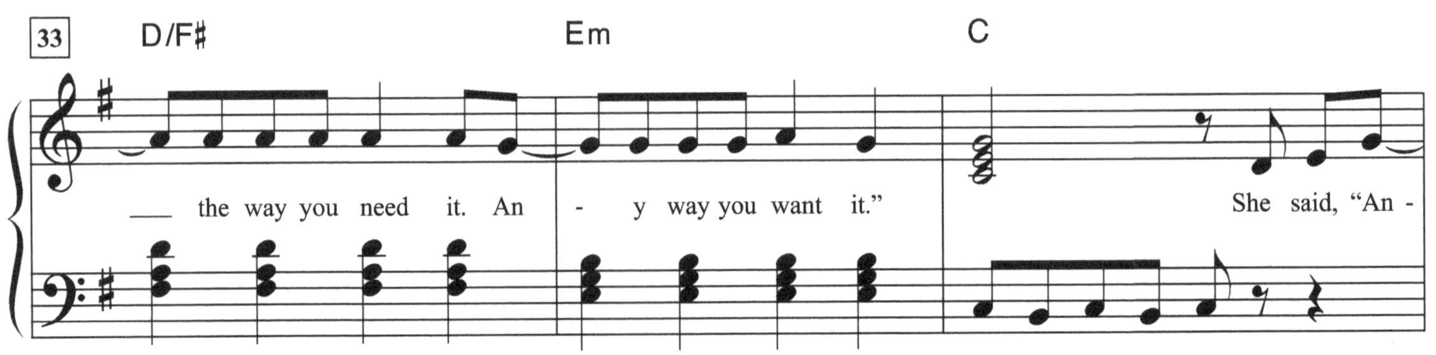
33
D/F♯
Em
C
the way you need it. An
- y way you want it."
She said, "An -

36
G
D/F♯
3
y way you want it. That's the way you need it. An -
1
3
5

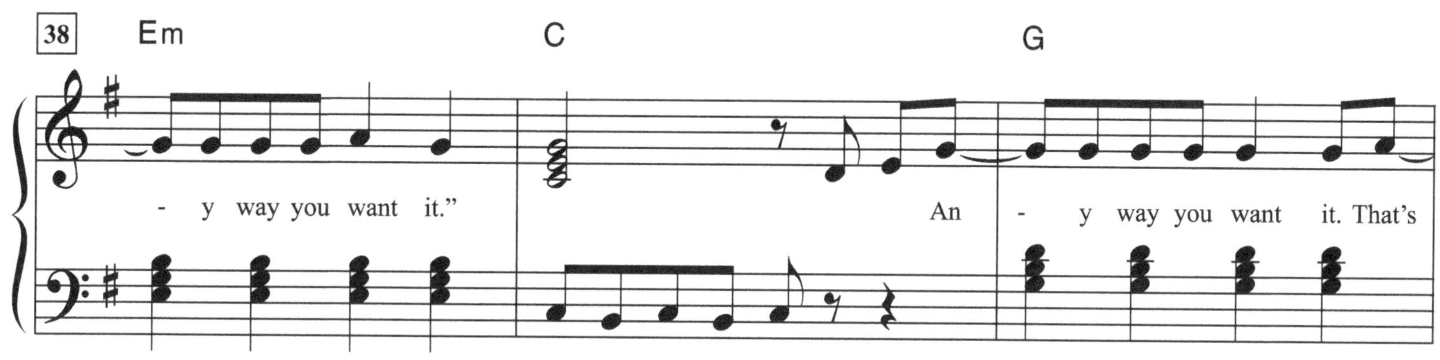
38
Em
C
G
- y way you want it."
An - y way you want it. That's

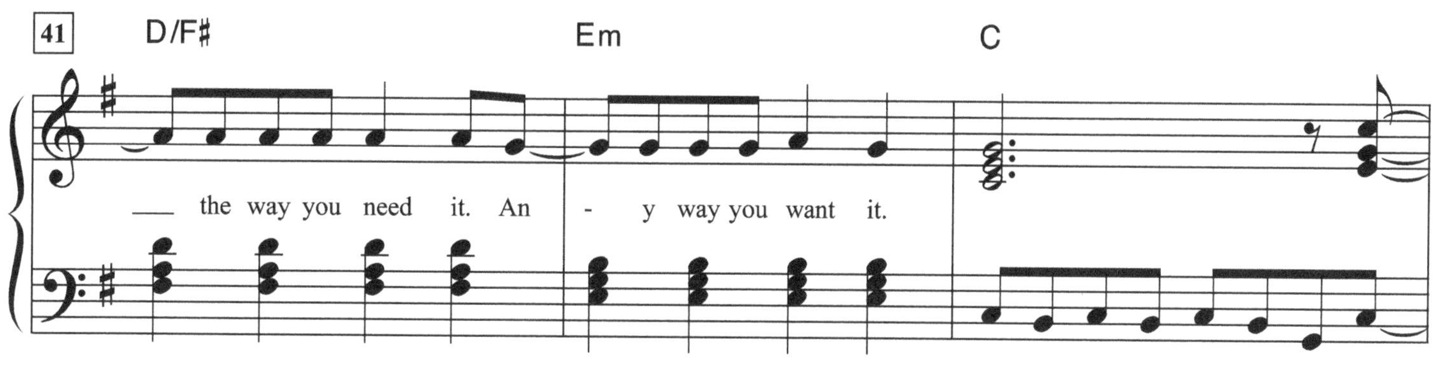
41
D/F♯
Em
C
the way you need it. An - y way you want it.

44
G
sfz

BRIDGE OVER TROUBLED WATER

Words and Music by Paul Simon
Arranged by Dan Coates

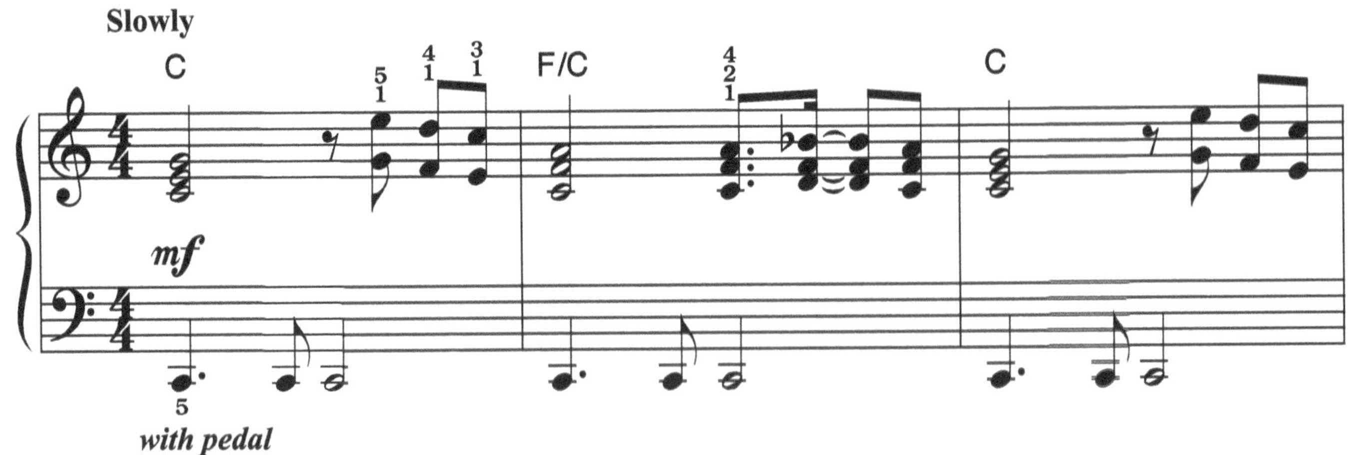

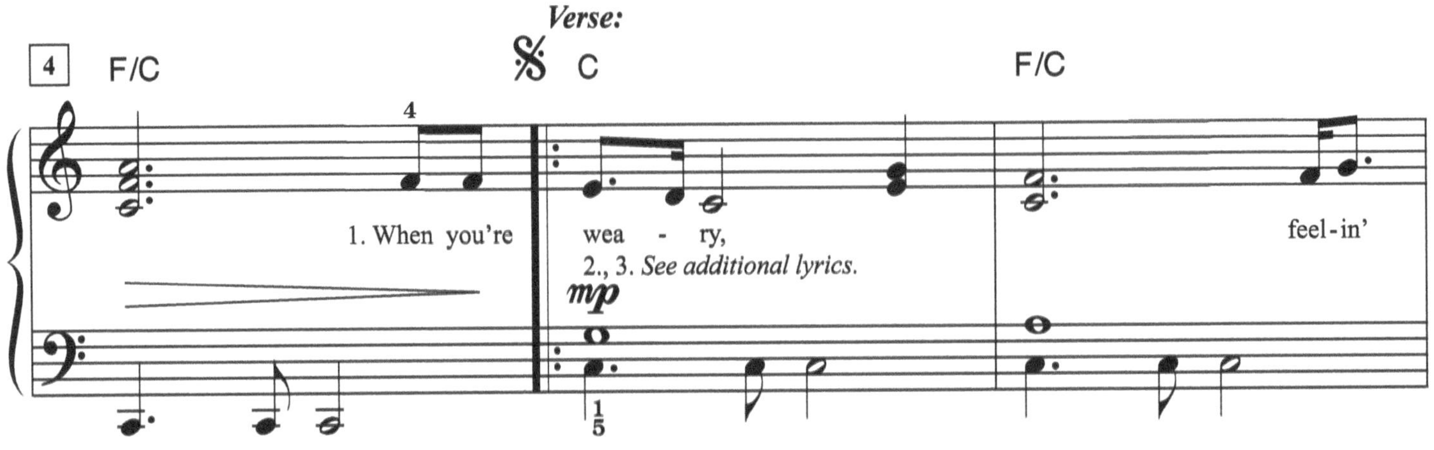

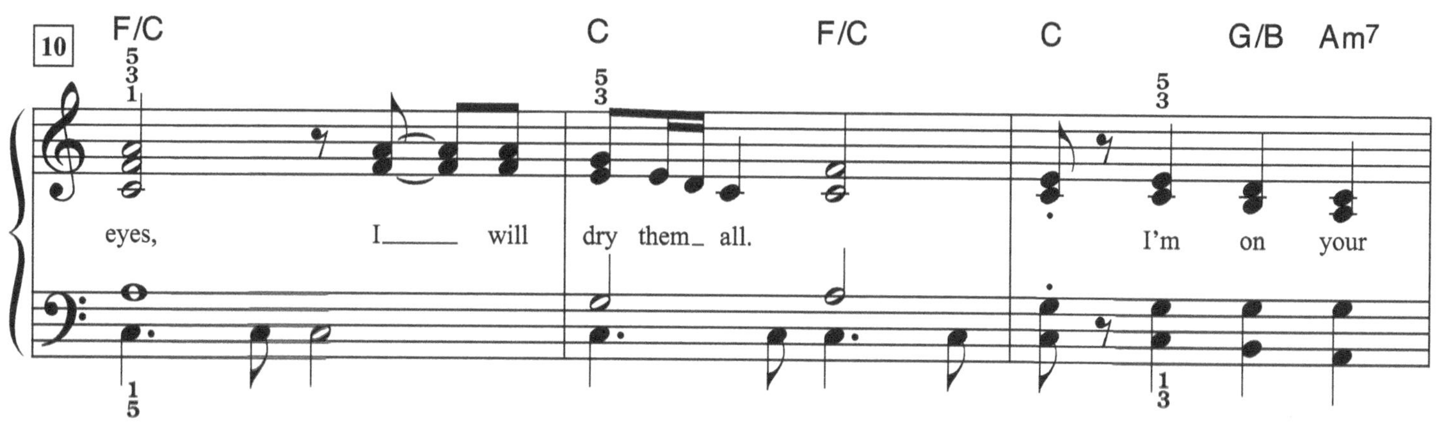
10
F/C
C
F/C
C
G/B
Am7
eyes, I will dry them all.
I'm on your

13
G
C
Cmaj7
side, oh, when times get rough.

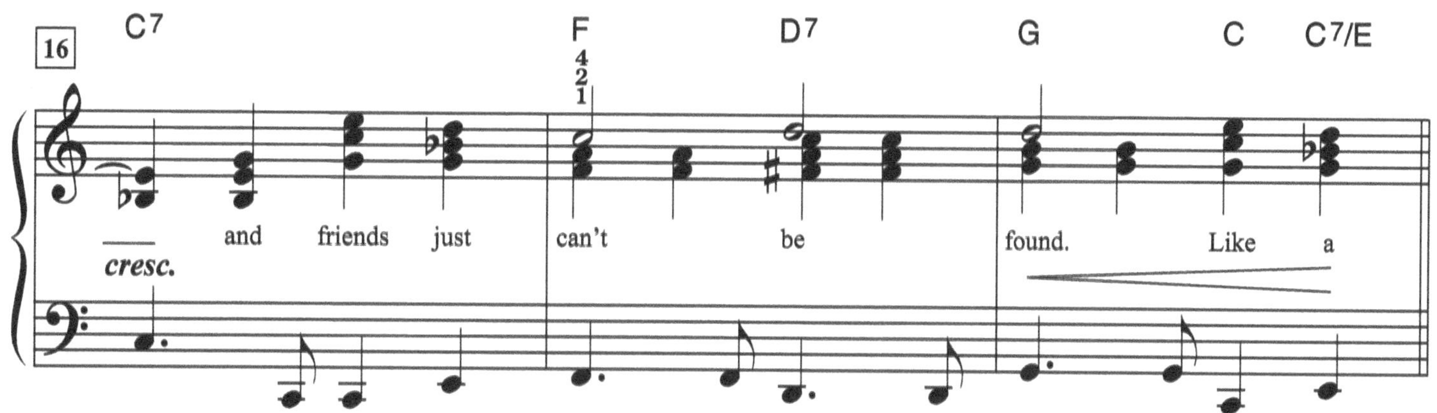
16
C7
F
D7
G
C
C7/E
and friends just can't be found. Like a
cresc.

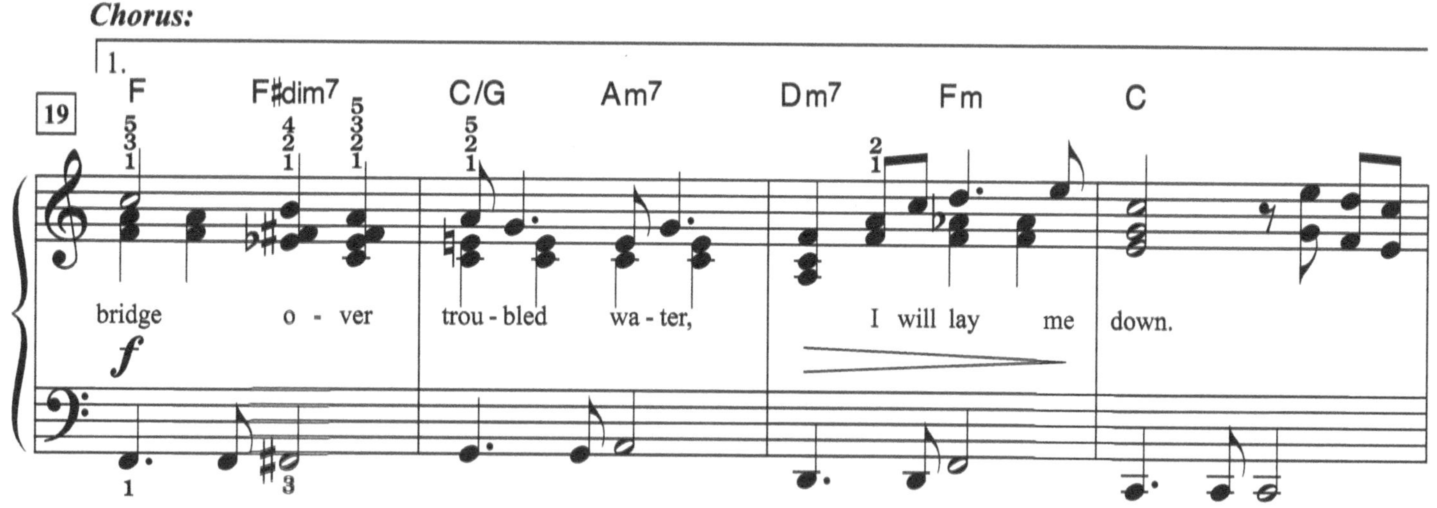
Chorus:
1.
19
F
F♯dim7
C/G
Am7
Dm7
Fm
C
bridge o - ver trou - bled wa - ter, I will lay me down.
f

23 F/C C F/C

2. When you're

Chorus:

2., 3.

26 F F♯dim7 C/G Am7 Dm7 E7

bridge o - ver trou - bled wa - ter, I will lay me

f

to Coda 𝄌

29 Am C7 F F♯dim7 C/G Am

down. Like a bridge o - ver trou - bled wa - ter,

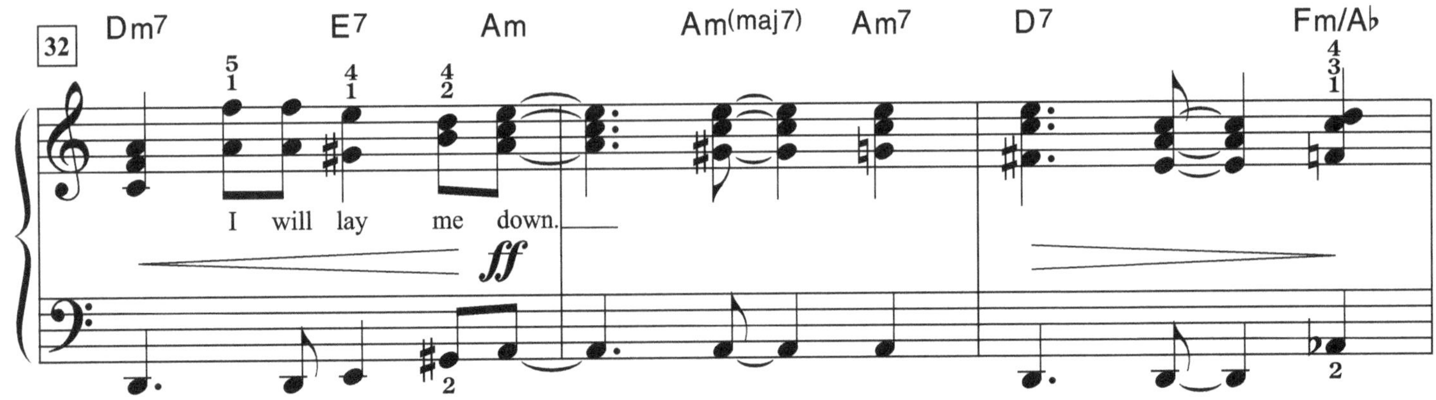

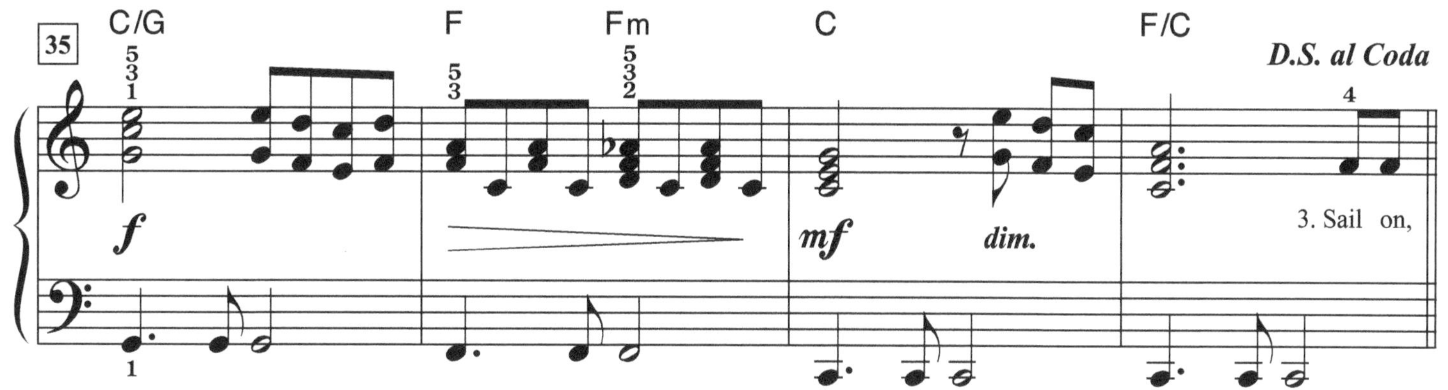

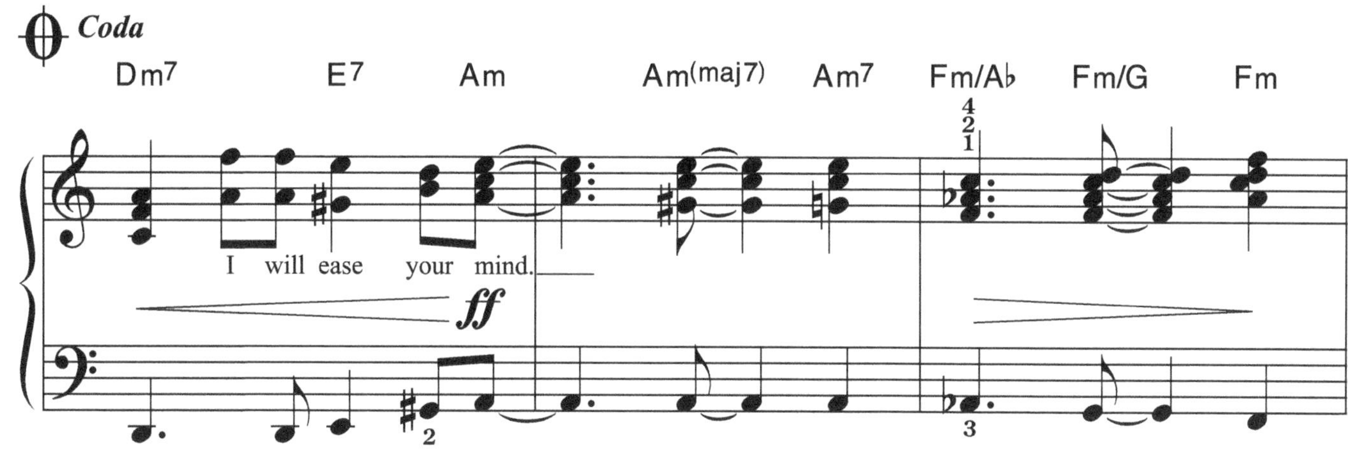

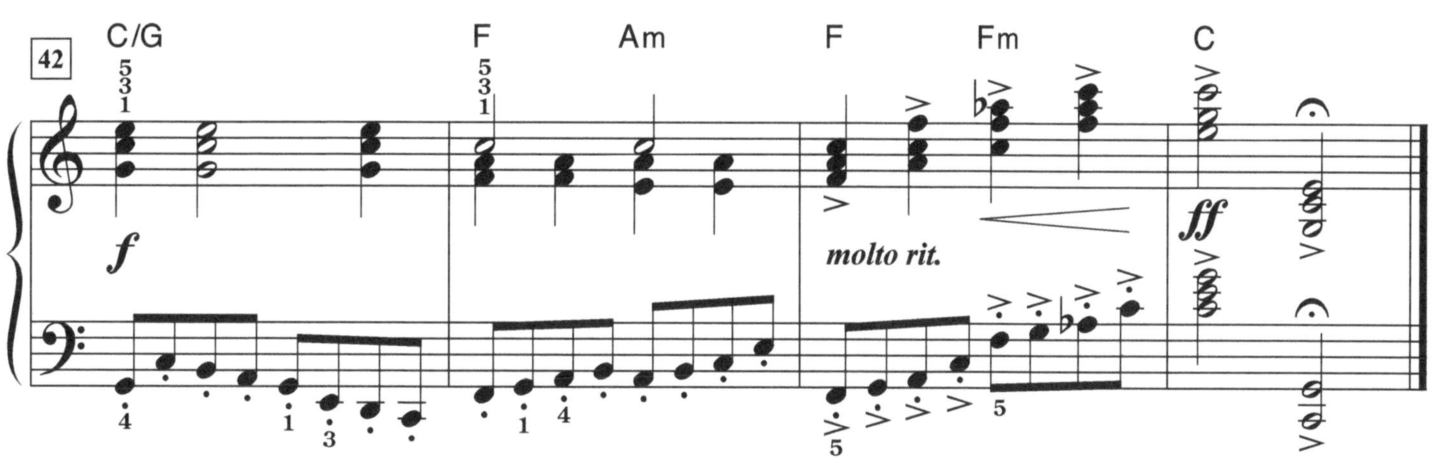

Verse 2:
When you're down and out,
When you're on the street,
When evening falls so hard, I will comfort you.
I'll take your part when darkness comes
And pain is all around.
Like a bridge over troubled water, I will lay me down.
Like a bridge over troubled water, I will lay me down.

Verse 3:
Sail on, silver girl, sail on by.
Your time has come to shine,
All your dreams are on their way.
See how they shine, if you need a friend.
I'm sailing right behind.
Like a bridge over troubled water, I will ease your mind.
Like a bridge over troubled water, I will ease your mind.

BEHIND BLUE EYES

Words and Music by Peter Townshend
Arranged by Dan Coates

13
C
A
fat - ed
to tell - ing
on - ly lies.

Chorus:

16
C
D
1., 2. But my
dreams,
they aren't as
mf

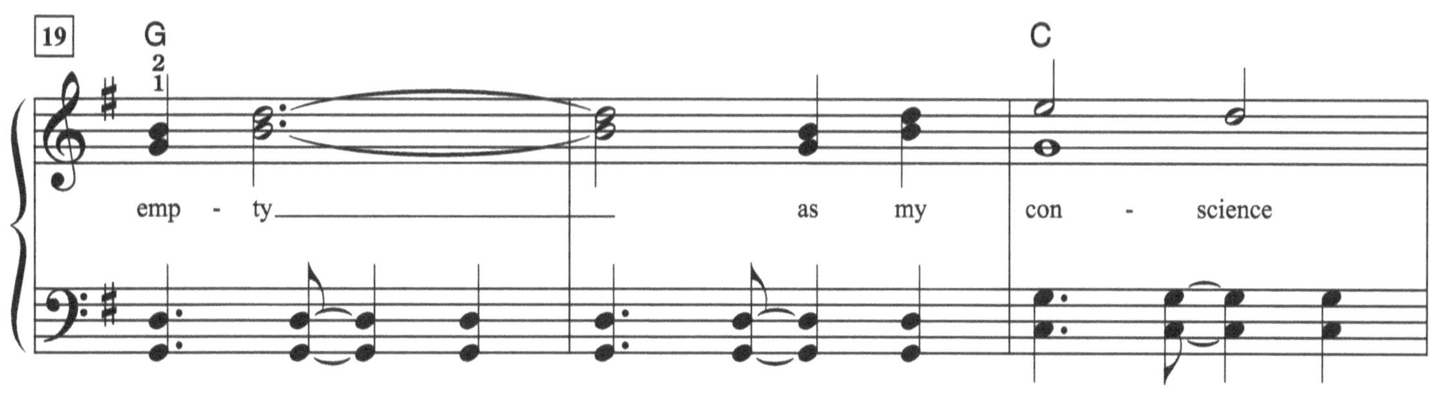
19
G
C
emp - ty
as my
con - science

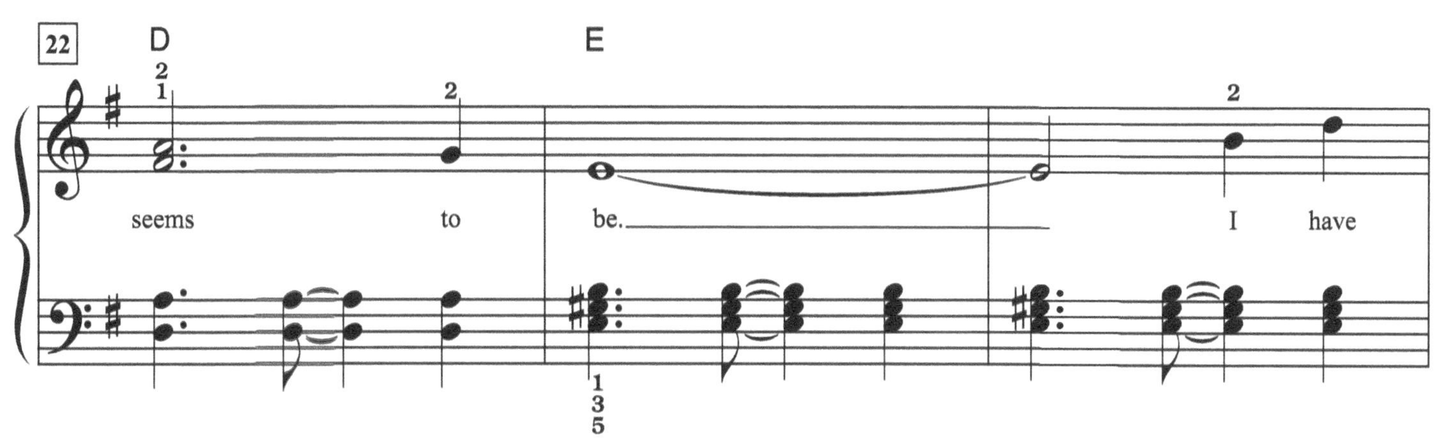
22
D
E
seems to
be.
I have

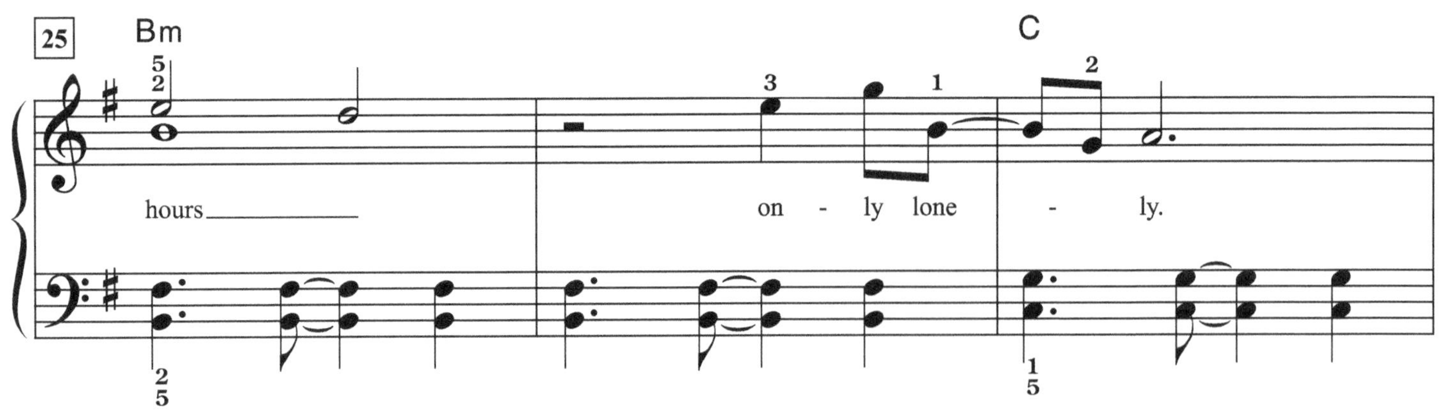
25
Bm
C
hours
on - ly lone - ly.

28
D
My love is venge - ance
that's nev - er

1.
2.
31
A
A
free.
free.

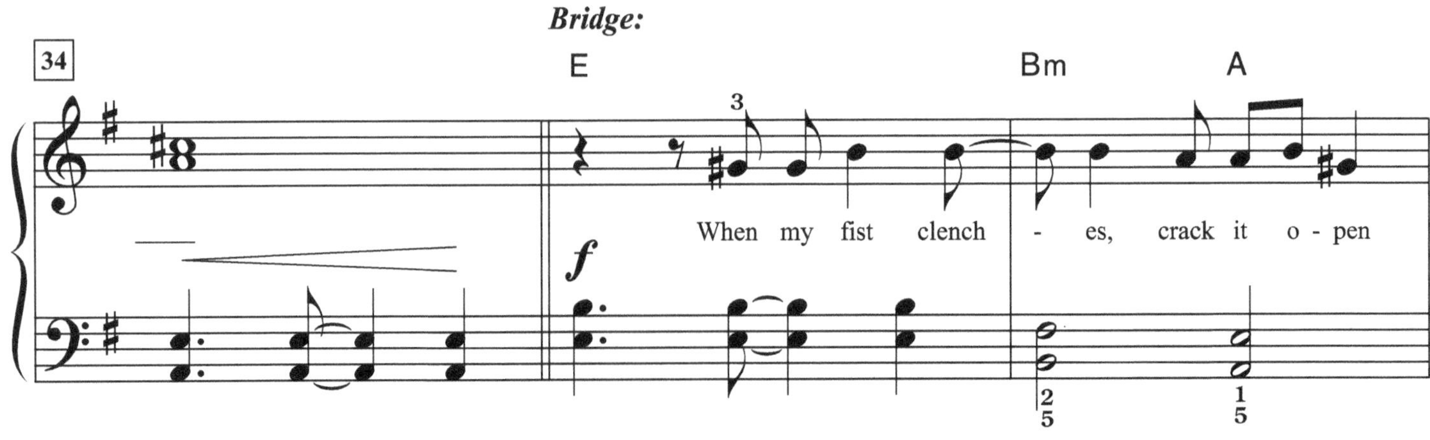
Bridge:
34
E
Bm
A
When my fist clench - es, crack it o - pen
f

37
E
Bm
G
D
be - fore I use it and lose my cool. When I smile,

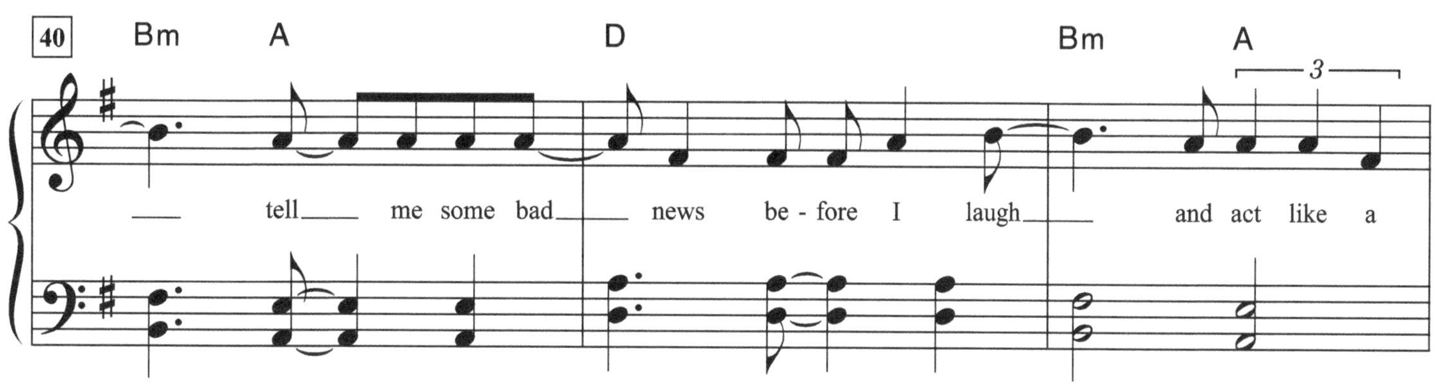
40
Bm
A
D
Bm
A
tell me some bad news be - fore I laugh and act like a

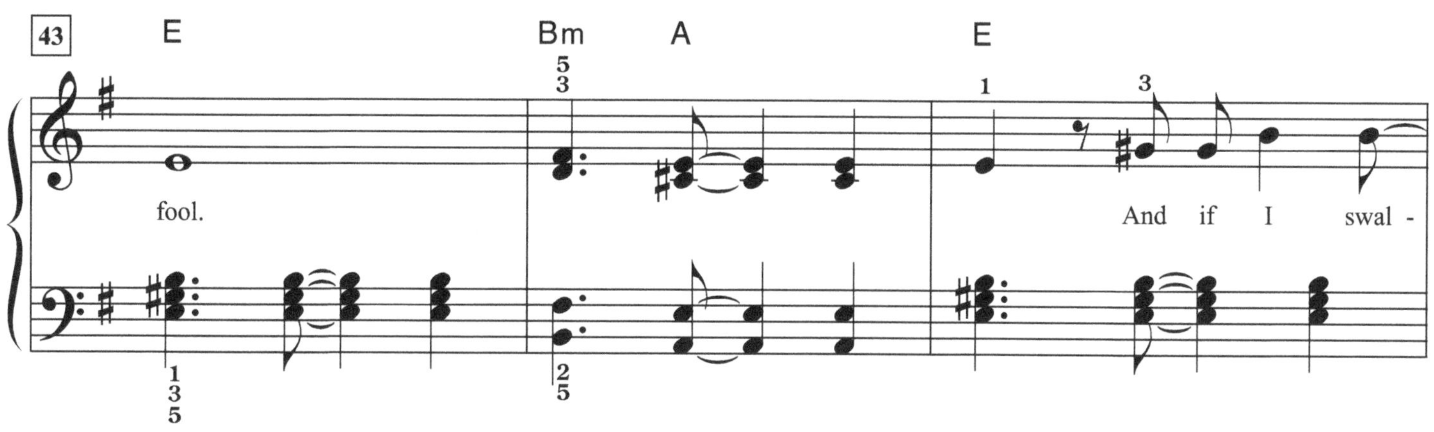
43
E
Bm
A
E
fool. And if I swal -

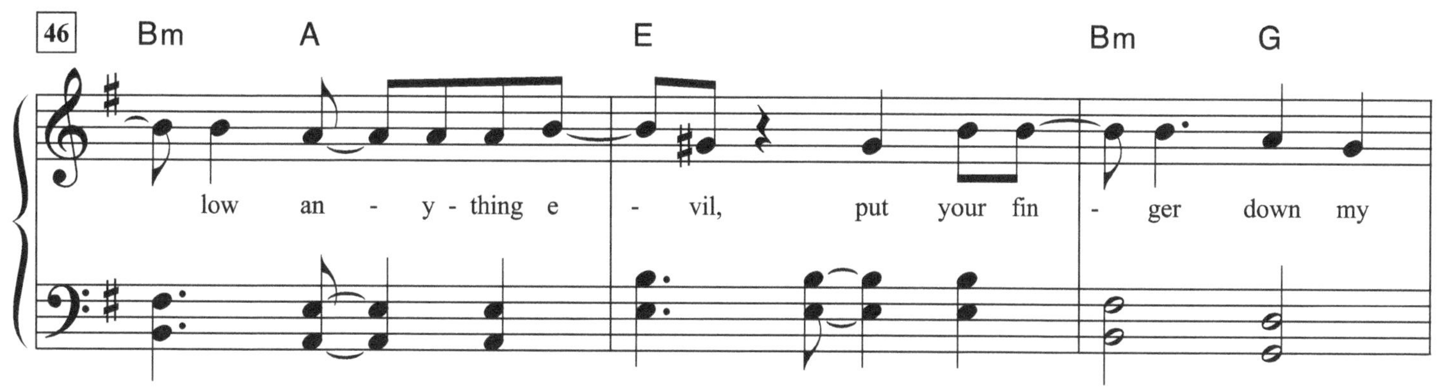
46
Bm
A
E
Bm
G
low an - y - thing e - vil, put your fin - ger down my

Verse 2:
No one knows what it's like to feel these feelings
Like I do. And I blame you!
No one bites back as hard on their anger.
None of my pain and woe
Can show through.
(To Chorus:)

DON'T STOP BELIEVIN'

Words and Music by Jonathan Cain,
Neal Schon and Steve Perry
Arranged by Dan Coates

15
1., 2., 4.
3., 5.
Am
B♭
Am
B♭
an - y - where.
an - y - where.
on and on and on and on.
19
F
Strang - ers
wait - ing,
up and down the
bou - le - vard, their
23
B♭
F
shad - ows
search - ing in the
night.
27
B♭
F
Street light
peo - ple,
liv-ing just to
find e - mo - tion,
31
B♭
C
F
C
F
B♭
to Coda
hid - ing
some - where in the
dark.

Verse 3:
A singer in a smoky room,
The smell of wine and cheap perfume.
For a smile they can share the night
It goes on and on and on and on.

Verse 4:
Working hard to get my fill.
Everybody wants a thrill,
Payin' anything to roll the dice
Just one more time.

Verse 5:
Some will win and some will lose,
Some were born to sing the blues.
Oh, the movie never ends,
It goes on and on and on and on.

DESPERADO

Words and Music by
Don Henley and Glenn Frey
Arranged by Dan Coates

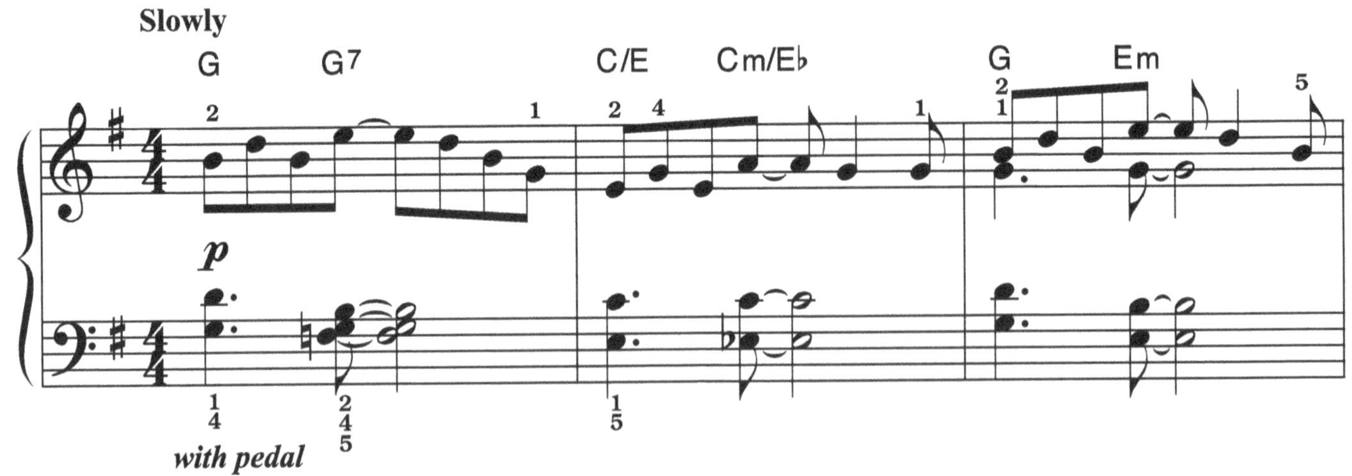

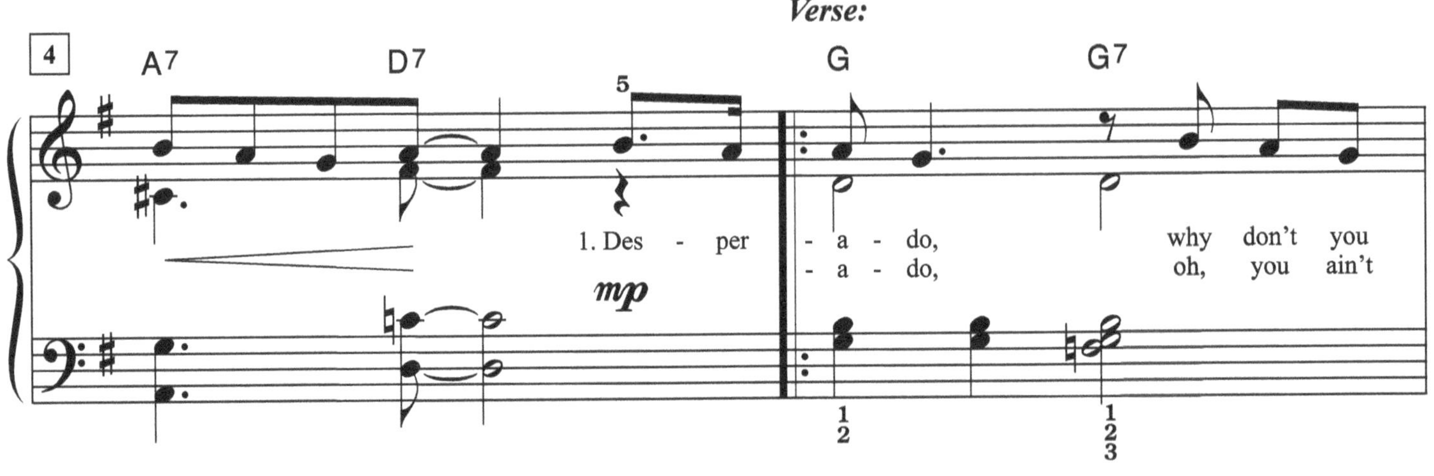

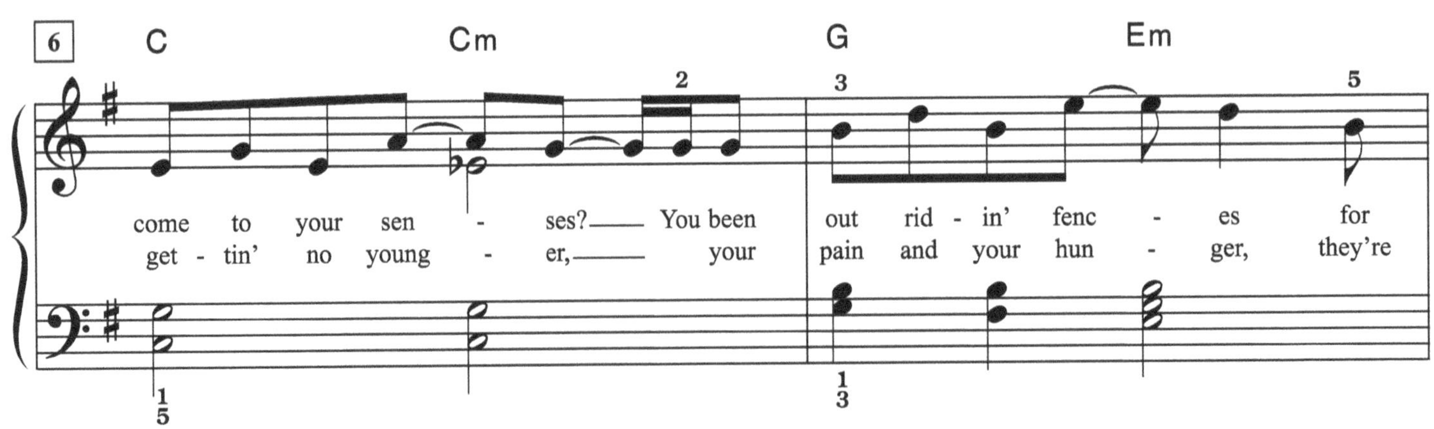

8
A D7 G G7
so long now. Oh, you're a hard one, I know that
driv - ing you home. And free - dom, well, that's just

10
C Cm G/D B7/D♯ Em
you got your rea - sons, these things that are pleas - in' you can
some peo - ple talk - in', your pris - on is walk - in' through this

12
A7 D7 G D/F♯ Em Bm7
hurt you some - how. Don't you draw the queen of dia - monds, boy, she'll
world all a - lone. Don't your feet get cold in the win - ter - time? The
cresc.
mf

15
C G Em C
beat you if she's a - ble, you know the queen of hearts is al - ways your best
sky won't snow and the sun won't shine, it's hard to tell the night - time from the

17
G D/F♯ Em Bm7
bet. Now it seems to me some fine things have been
day. You're los - in' all your highs and lows. Ain't it
19
C G Em A7
1.
laid up - on your ta - ble, but you on - ly want the ones that you can't
fun - ny how the feel - in' goes a -
21
Am7/D D7 Am7 Am7/D D7
2.
get. 2. Des - per way? 3. Des - per -
mp
mp
24
G G7 C Cm G Em
a - do, why don't you come to your sens - es? Come down from your fenc - es,

27
A
D7
G
F/A
G/B
o - pen the gate. It may be rain - in', but there's a

29
C
Cm
G
Em
G/D
rain - bow a - bove you. You bet - ter let some - bod - y - love you,
mf

31
C
G/B
Am7
G/D
B7/D♯
Em
let some - bod - y love you, you bet - ter let some - bod - y love you be -
f

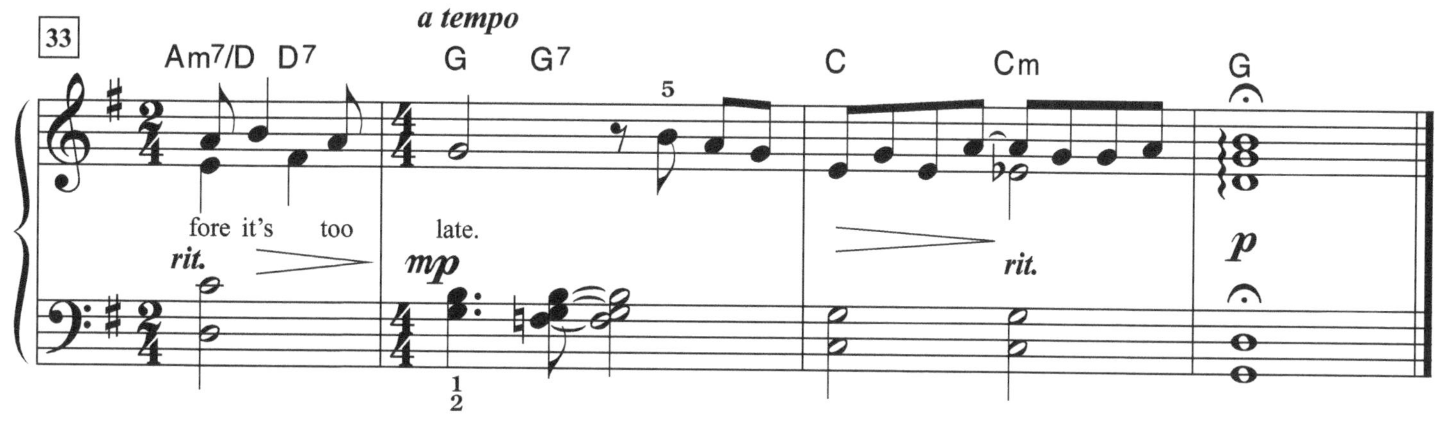
33
a tempo
Am7/D
D7
G
G7
C
Cm
G
fore it's too late.
rit.
mp
rit.
p

GIMME SOME LOVIN'

Words and Music by Steve Winwood,
Muff Winwood and Spencer Davis
Arranged by Dan Coates

Moderately, with a steady beat

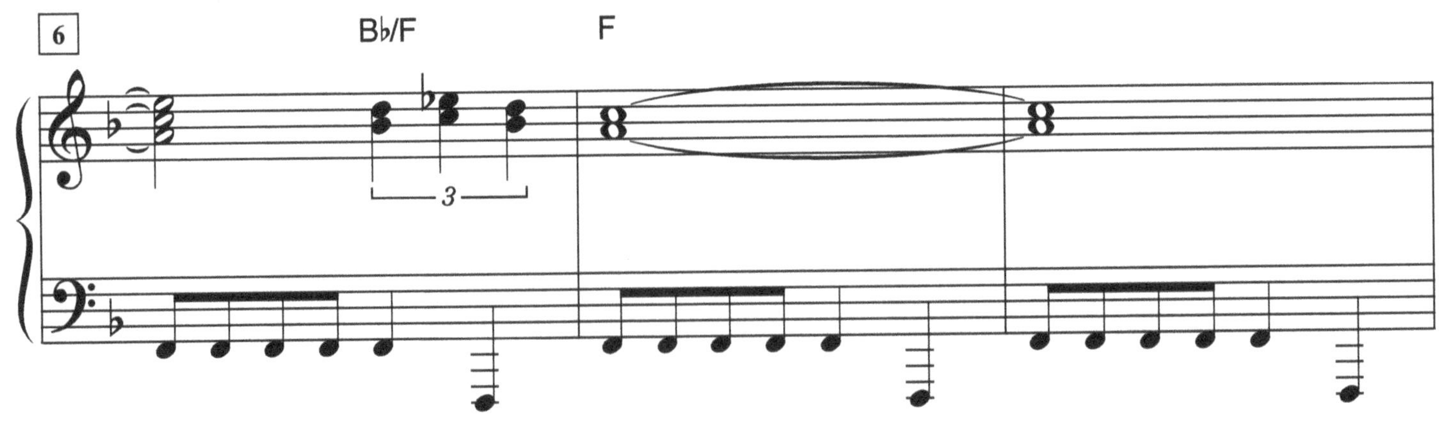

9
F
B♭/F
F7
B♭/F
Verse:
Fm
B♭/F
mf
1. Well, my
tem-p'ra-ture's ris - ing and my
feel so good; ev - 'ry -
feel so good; ev - 'ry -

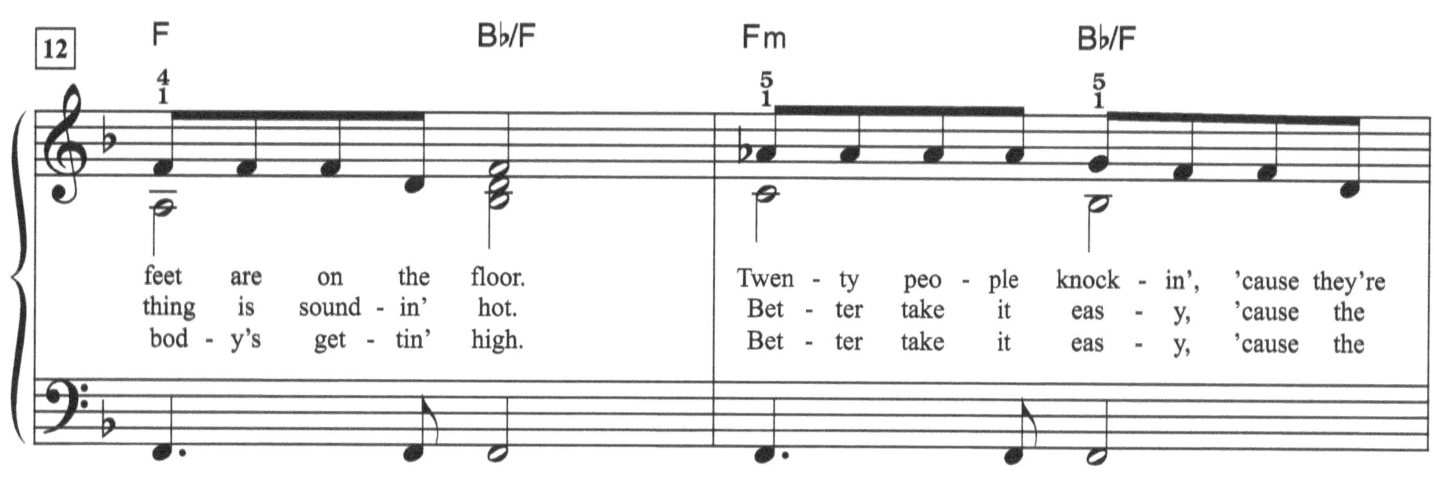
12
F
B♭/F
Fm
B♭/F
feet are on the floor.
thing is sound - in' hot.
bod - y's get - tin' high.
Twen - ty peo - ple knock - in', 'cause they're
Bet - ter take it eas - y, 'cause the
Bet - ter take it eas - y, 'cause the

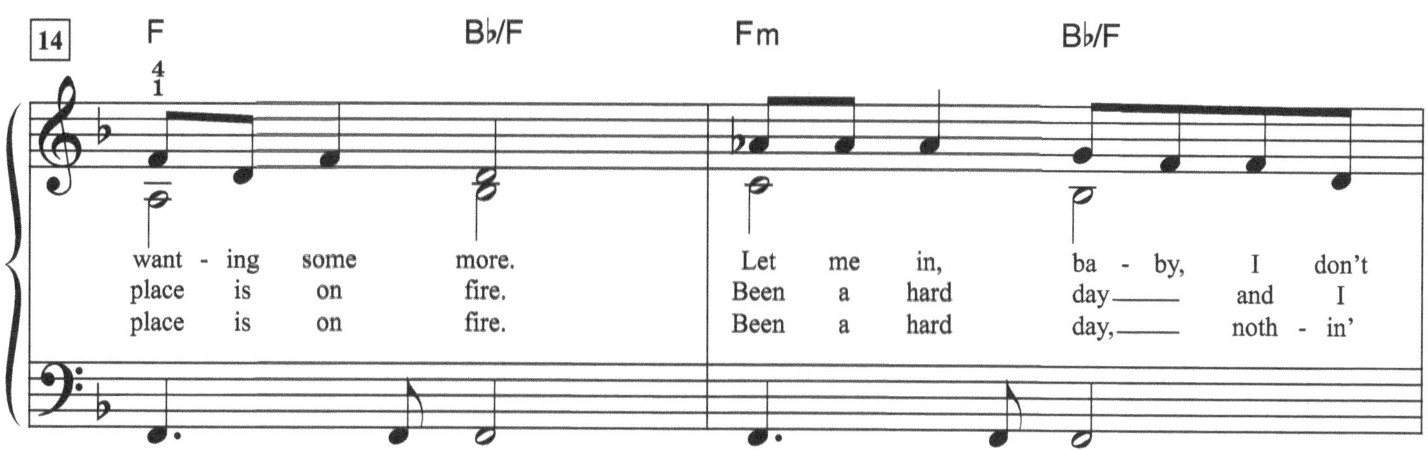
14
F
B♭/F
Fm
B♭/F
want - ing some more.
place is on fire.
place is on fire.
Let me in, ba - by, I don't
Been a hard day and I
Been a hard day, noth - in'

16
F
B♭/F
Fm
B♭/F
Fm
know what you've got. But you'd bet - ter take it eas - y. This
don't know what to do. Wait a min - ute, ba - by. It could
went too good. Now I'm gon - na re - lax, hon - ey. Ev -

18
B♭/F
Chorus:
Fm
place is hot.
hap - pen to you.
'ry - bod - y should.
So glad we made

20
A♭
B♭7
D♭
it, so glad we made it. You got - ta

23
F
Bb/F
F
f
gim - me some
lov - in',
gim - me some
26
Bb/F
to Coda
F
Bb/F
lov - in',
gim - me some
lov - in' ev - er - y
29
F
F7
day.
cresc.
ff
32
Bb/F
F
3

35
1.
2.
F7
Bb/F
D.S. al Coda
2. Well, I
3. Well, I
Coda
F
gim-me some
lov - in', (gim-me some
lov - in') gim-me some
41
lov - in', (gim-me some
lov - in') gim-me some
lov - in' ev - er - y
day.
rit.

GREAT BALLS OF FIRE

Words and Music by
Otis Blackwell and Jack Hammer
Arranged by Dan Coates

12
G
F7
moved me, hon - ey.
I changed my mind,
love's just fine.
15
C
F7
Good - ness gra - cious, great balls of fire!
Kiss me, ba - by.
18
C7
Hmm,
it feels good.
21
F7
G7
Hold me, ba - by.
I want to love you like a
24
lov - er should.
You're fine,
so kind.
cresc.

27
C
I've got to tell this world you're mine, mine, mine.
I chew my nails and I

30
F7
twid - dle my thumbs.
I'm real ner - vous, but it sure is fun.

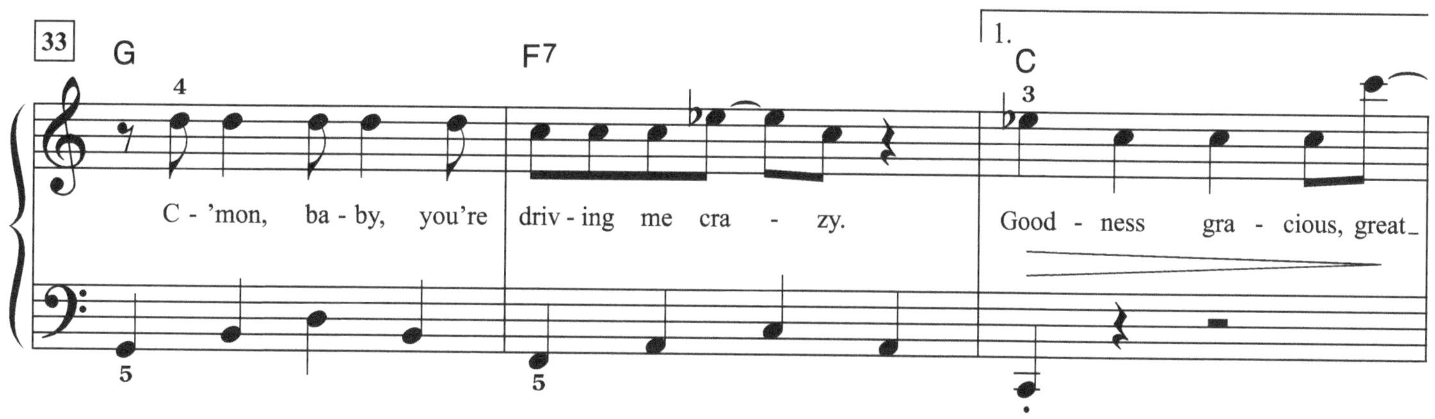
33
G
F7
1.
C
C - 'mon, ba - by, you're driv - ing me cra - zy.
Good - ness gra - cious, great

36
2.
C
balls of fire!
Good-ness gra-cious, great balls of fire!

HOTEL CALIFORNIA

Words and Music by Don Henley,
Glenn Frey and Don Felder
Arranged by Dan Coates

15
D
D7
Fmaj7
ris - ing up through the air.
that she calls friends.
Up a - head in the
How they dance in the
18
C
dis - tance, I saw a shim - mer - ing light.
court - yard; sweet sum - mer sweat.
21
Dm
E
My head grew heav - y and my sight grew dim; I had to stop for the
Some dance to re - mem - ber; some dance to for -
24
E7
Am
night. There she stood in the door - way;
get. So I called up the cap - tain:
27
E
E7
G
I heard the mis - sion bell. And I was think - ing
"Please bring me my wine." He said, "We have - n't had that

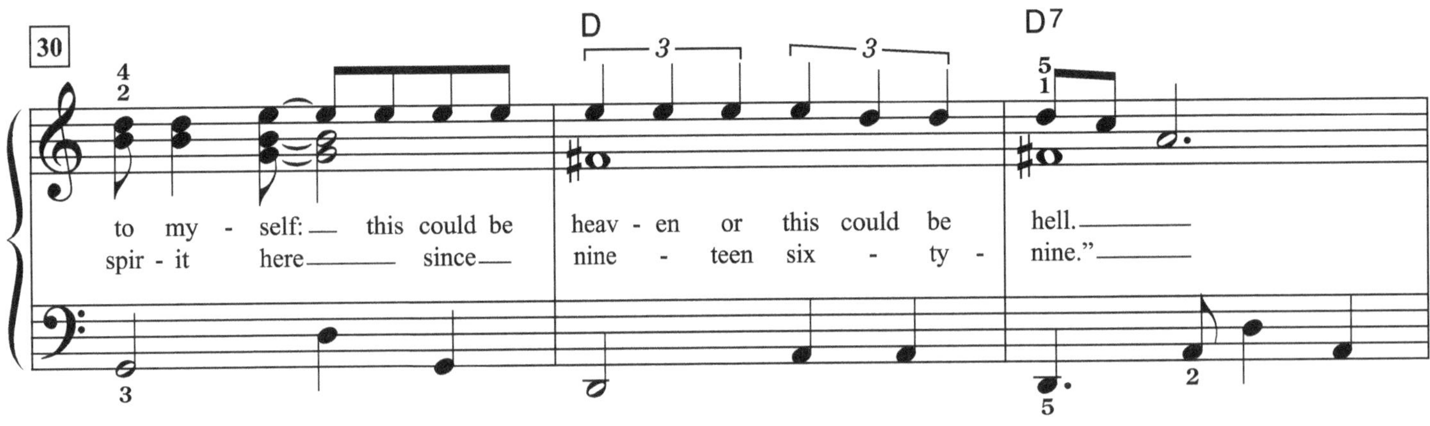
30
D
D7
to my - self: this could be
heav - en or this could be
hell.
spir - it here since
nine - teen six - ty -
nine."

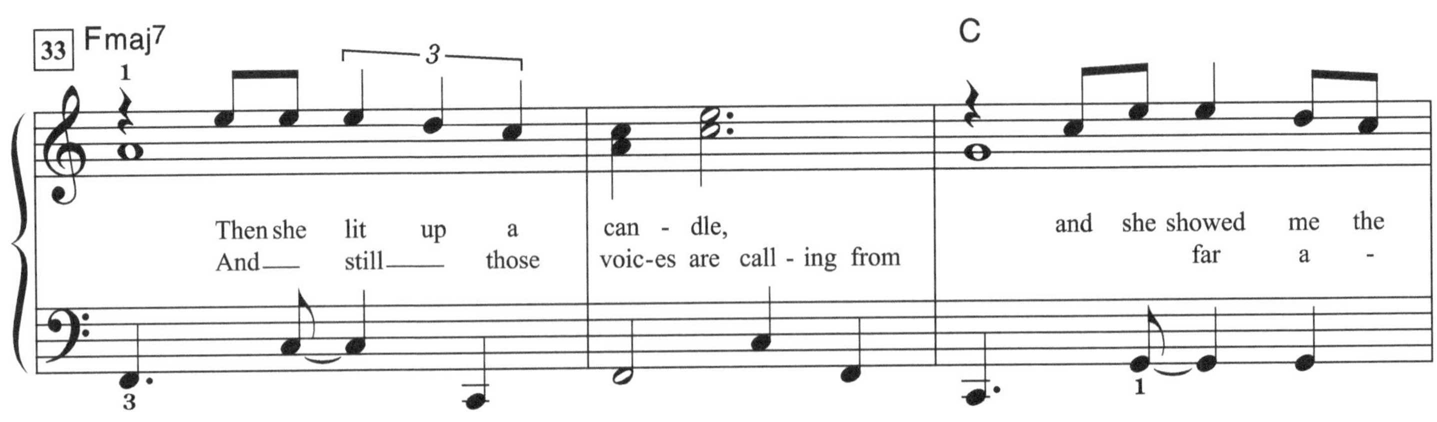
33 Fmaj7
C
Then she lit up a
can - dle,
and she showed me the
And still those
voic-es are call - ing from
far a -

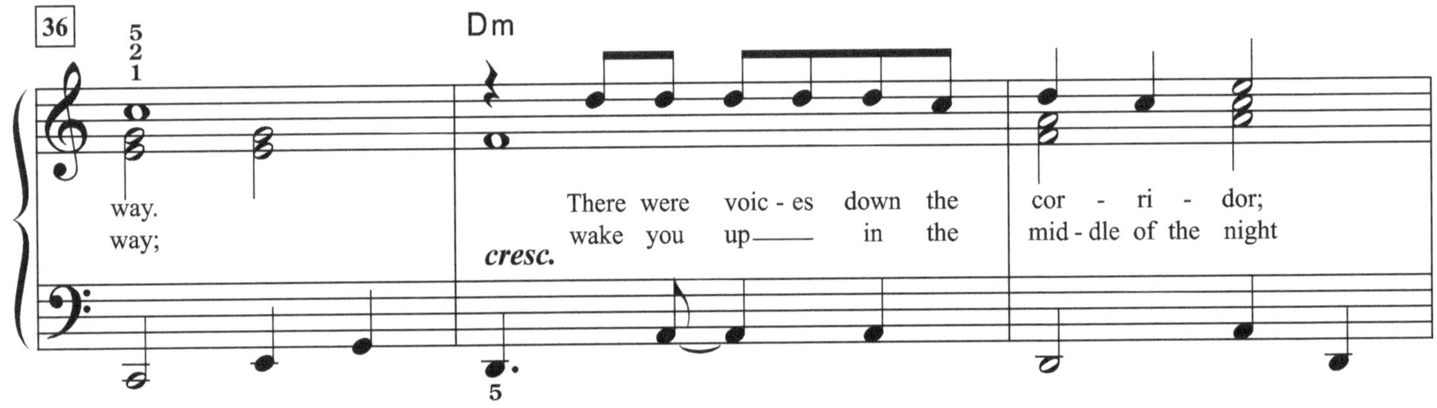
36
Dm
way.
way;
There were voic - es down the
cor - ri - dor;
cresc.
wake you up in the
mid - dle of the night

Chorus:
39 E
F
I thought I heard them
say:
"Wel - come to the
just to hear them
say:
"Wel - come to the

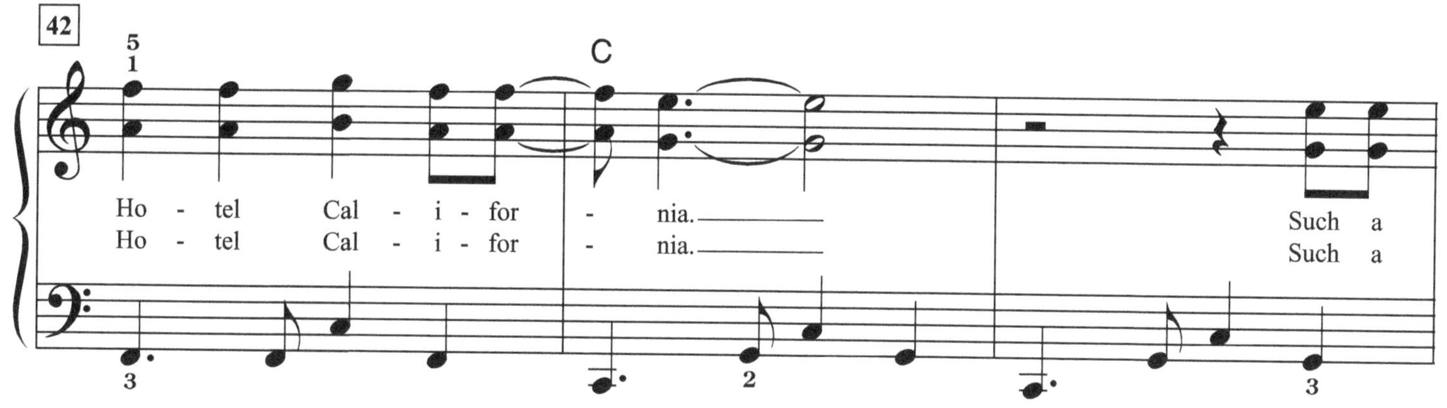
42
C
Ho - tel Cal - i - for - nia.
Ho - tel Cal - i - for - nia.
Such a
Such a

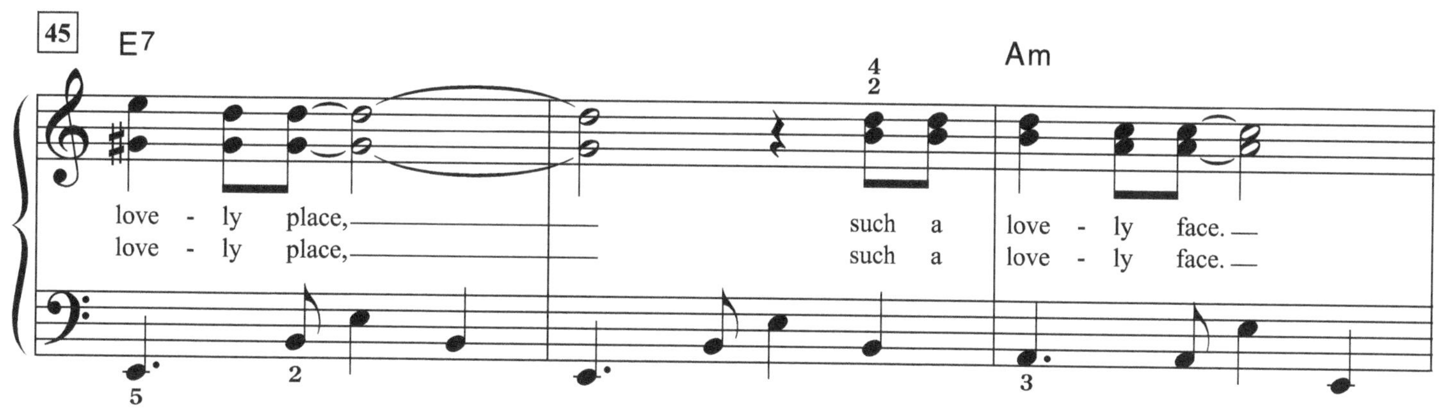
45
E7
Am
love - ly place,
love - ly place,
such a
such a
love - ly face.
love - ly face.

48
F
They're
Plen - ty of room at the
liv - in' it up at the
Ho - tel Cal - i - for -
Ho - tel Cal - i - for -

51
C
Dm
nia.
nia.
An - y - time of year,
What a nice sur - prise;

54
to Coda
1.
E
you can find it here."
bring your

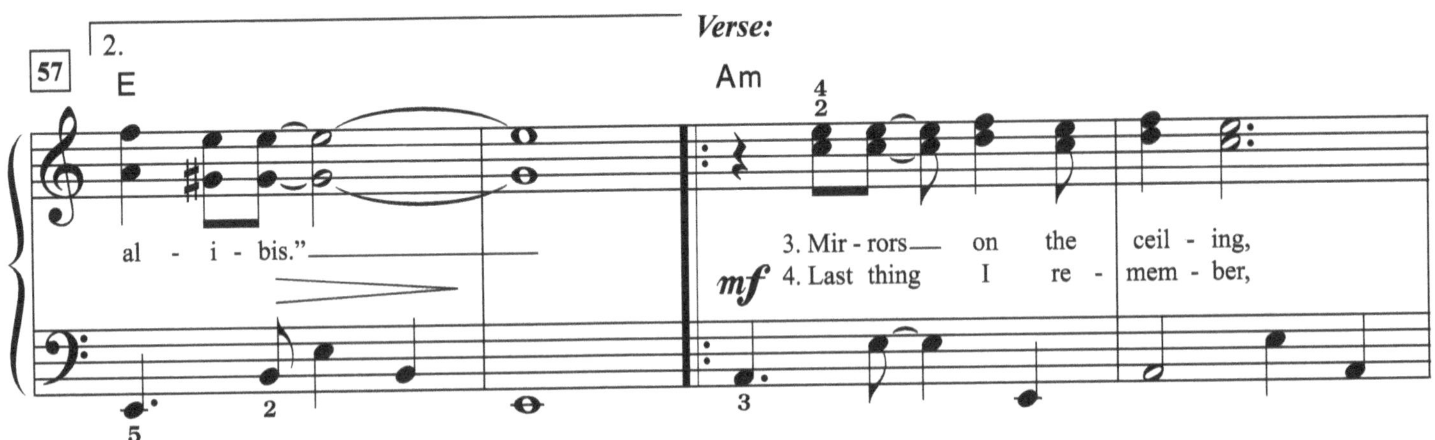
57
2.
E
Verse:
Am
al - i - bis."
3. Mir - rors on the ceil - ing,
mf
4. Last thing I re - mem - ber,

61
E
E7
G
the pink cham - pagne on ice, and she said "We are all just
I was run - ning for the door. I had to find the

64
D
pris - on - ers here of our own de - vice."
pas - sage back to the place I was be - fore.

67
Fmaj7
C
And in the mas - ter's chamb - bers,
"Re - lax," said the night man.
they gath - ered for the
"We are pro - grammed to re -

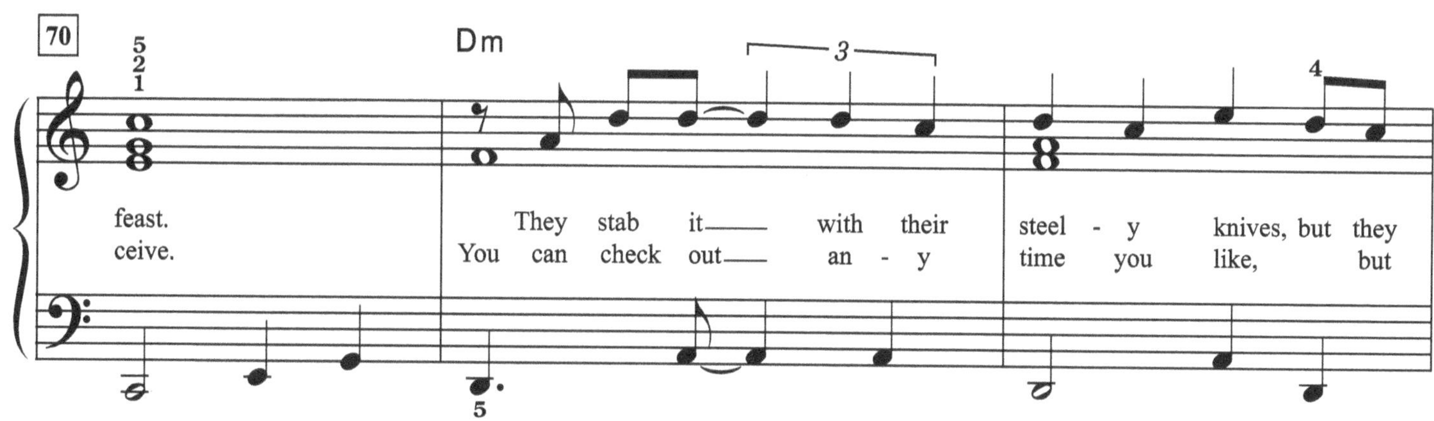
70
Dm
feast.
ceive.
They stab it with their
You can check out an - y
steel - y knives, but they
time you like, but

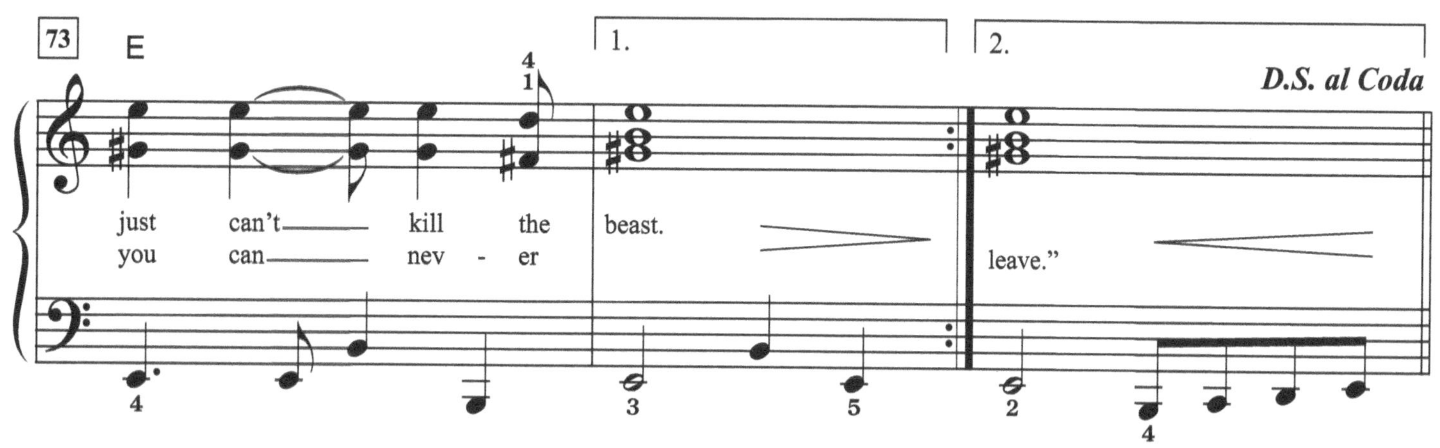
73
E
1.
2.
D.S. al Coda
just can't kill the
you can nev - er
beast.
leave."

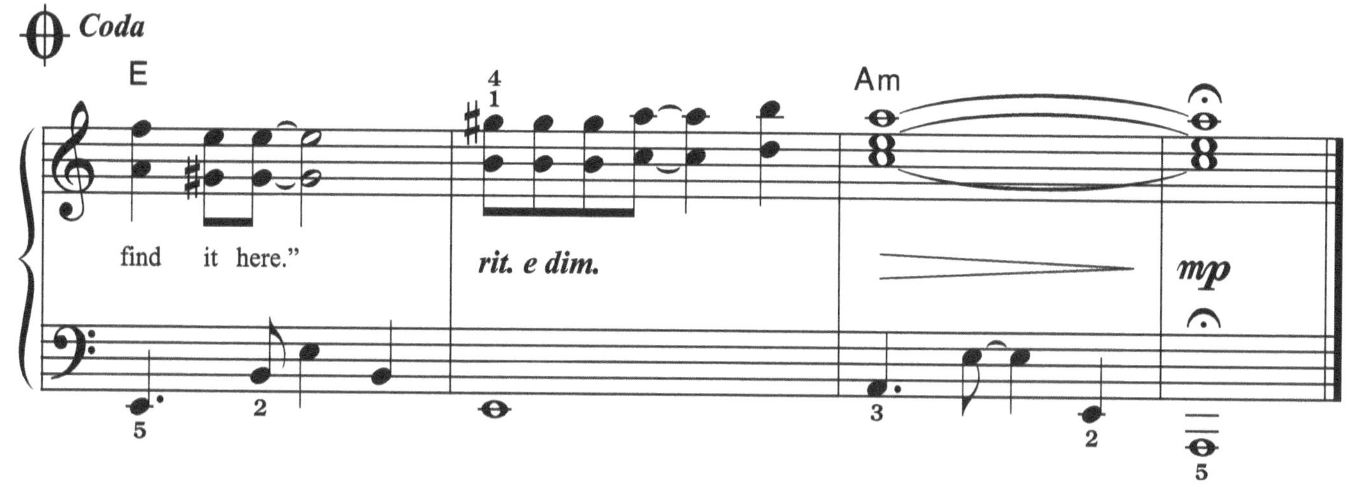
Coda
E
Am
find it here."
rit. e dim.
mp

HOW DEEP IS YOUR LOVE

Words and Music by Barry Gibb,
Maurice Gibb and Robin Gibb
Arranged by Dan Coates

13
B♭
Am7
Gm7
to me on a sum - mer breeze, keep me warm in your love, then you soft -
not think I care for you, when you know down in - side that I real -
to me on a sum - mer breeze, keep me warm in your love then you soft -

16
E♭
Am7
B♭/C
- ly leave.
- ly do.
- ly leave.
And it's me you need to show: How deep
mf

Chorus:

19
F
Fmaj7
B♭maj7
is your love, how deep is your love? I real - ly mean to learn.

22
B♭m
F
Cm/E♭
'Cause we're liv - ing in a world of fools, break - ing us

25
D7
Gm
to Coda
down when they all should let us be. We be - long
1., 2.
3.
28
B♭m
B♭m
F
Am7
B♭/C
to you and
to you and me. Na na na na na.
mp
31
D.S. al Coda
Coda
B♭m
How deep
mf
to you and
34
F
Fmaj7
B♭maj7
F
me.
rit. e dim.
p

IMAGINE

Words and Music by John Lennon
Arranged by Dan Coates

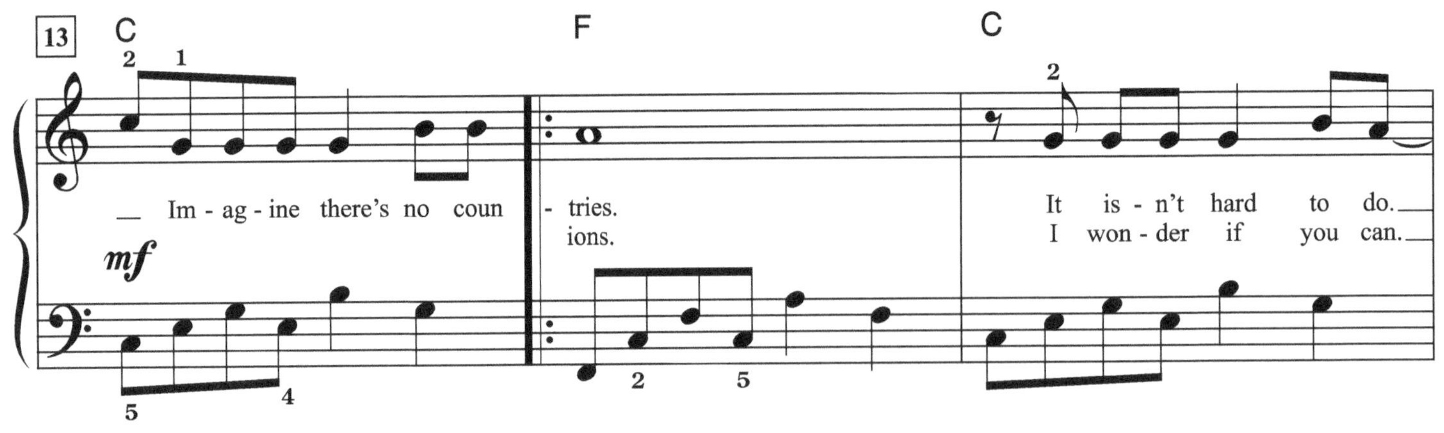
13
C
F
C
mf
Im - ag - ine there's no coun - tries.
ions.
It is - n't hard to do.
I won - der if you can.

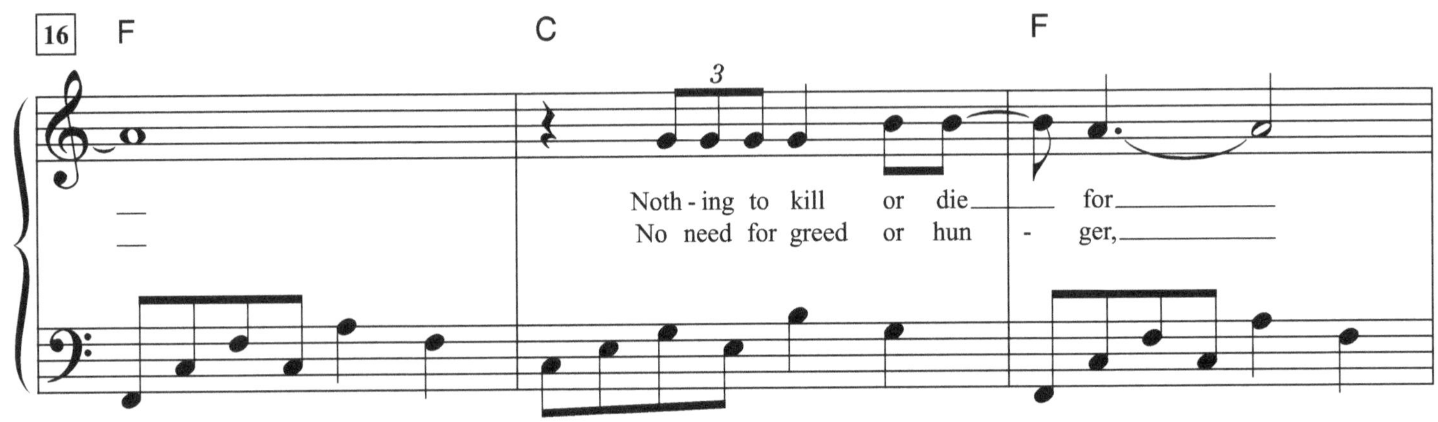
16
F
C
F
Noth - ing to kill or die for
No need for greed or hun - ger,

19
C
F
Am/E
and no re - li - gion, too.
a broth - er - hood of man.
Im - ag - ine all the peo -
Im - ag - ine all the peo -

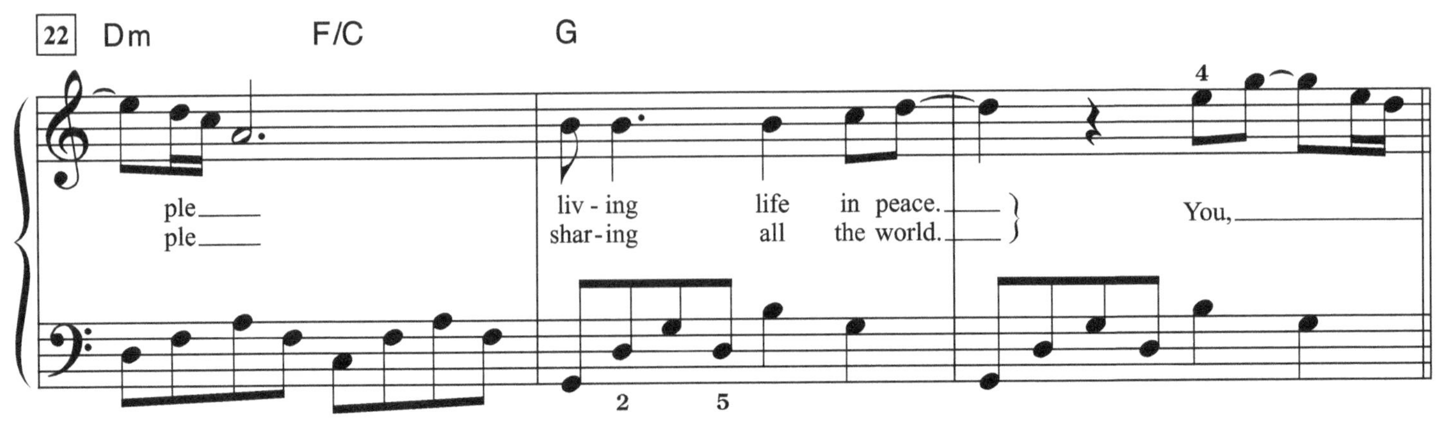
22
Dm
F/C
G
ple
ple
liv - ing life in peace.
shar - ing all the world.
You,

Chorus:
25
F
G
C
E7
you may say I'm a
dream - er.
But I'm not the on - ly
28
one.
I hope some day you'll
join us
31
1.
and the world will
be as one.
Im - ag - ine no pos - ses -
34
2.
and the world will
live as one.

I SAW HER STANDING THERE

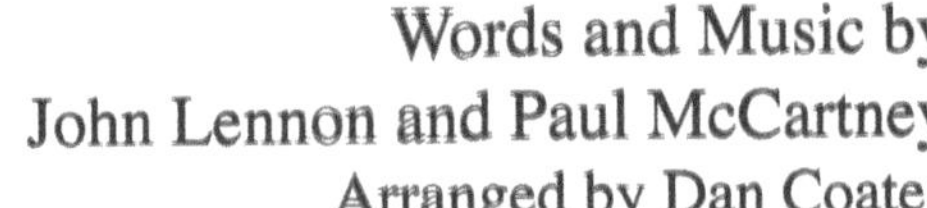
Words and Music by
John Lennon and Paul McCartney
Arranged by Dan Coates

Fast rock

C7 | 1. | 2.

mf

1. Well, she was

Verse:

4 C7 F7

just sev - en - teen, and you know what I
she looked at me and I, I could

7 C7

mean. And the way she looked__ was way be - yond com -
see that be - fore too long__ I fell in love with

10 G7 C

pare.__ So how could I
her.__ She would - n't

13
C7
F
Fm
dance with an - oth - er,
woah, when I
dance with an - oth - er,
woah, when I

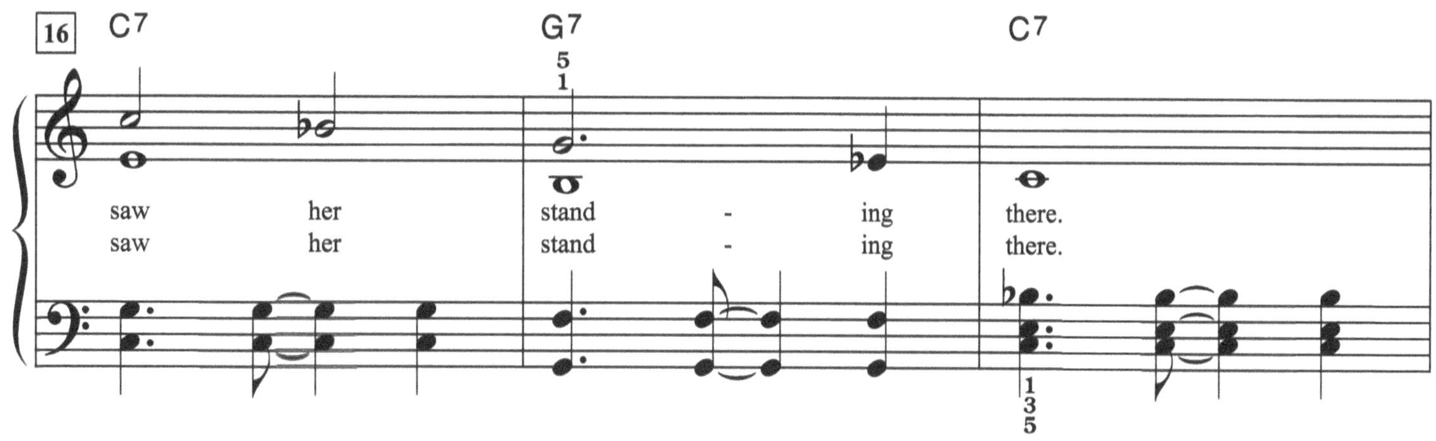
16
C7
G7
C7
saw her stand - ing there.
saw her stand - ing there.

19
1.
2.
Bridge:
F7
2. Well,
Well, my
heart went boom

22
when I crossed the room, and I

25
G
held her hand in mine.

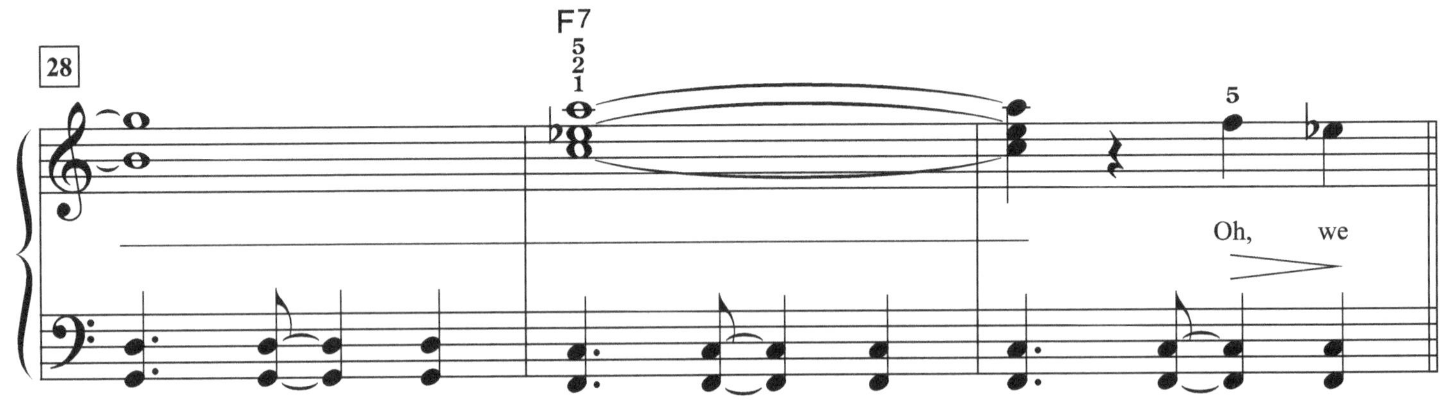
28
F7
Oh, we

Verse:
31
C7
F7
danced through the night and we held each oth - er
mf

34
C7
tight. And be - fore too long, I fell in love with

37
G7
her.
Now,
C
I'll
nev - er
40
C7
dance
with
an -
F
oth - er,
Fm
ooh,
since I
43
C7
saw
her
G7
stand
-
ing
C7
there.
46
Oh,
since I
saw
her
G7
stand
-
ing
49
F7
there.
C7
C7(add9)

KILLING ME SOFTLY

Words and Music by
Charles Fox and Norman Gimbel
Arranged by Dan Coates

Chorus:
13
Am
Dm
G
Strum-ming my pain with his fin - gers,
sing-ing my life with his
mf
16
C
Am
D
words.
Kill-ing me soft - ly with his song,
kill-ing me soft -
19
G
F
C
ly with his song.
Tell-ing my whole life with his
22
F
B♭
words,
kill-ing me soft - ly with his
1., 2.
3.
25
A
A
song.
song.
rit. e dim.

MOONDANCE

Words and Music by Van Morrison
Arranged by Dan Coates

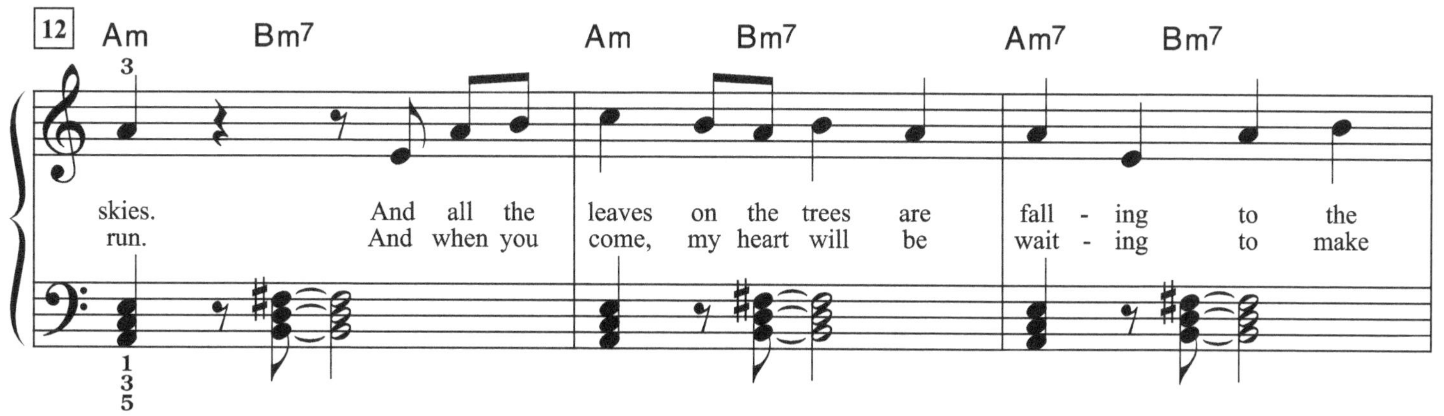
12
Am
Bm7
Am
Bm7
Am7
Bm7
skies. And all the leaves on the trees are fall - ing to the
run. And when you come, my heart will be wait - ing to make

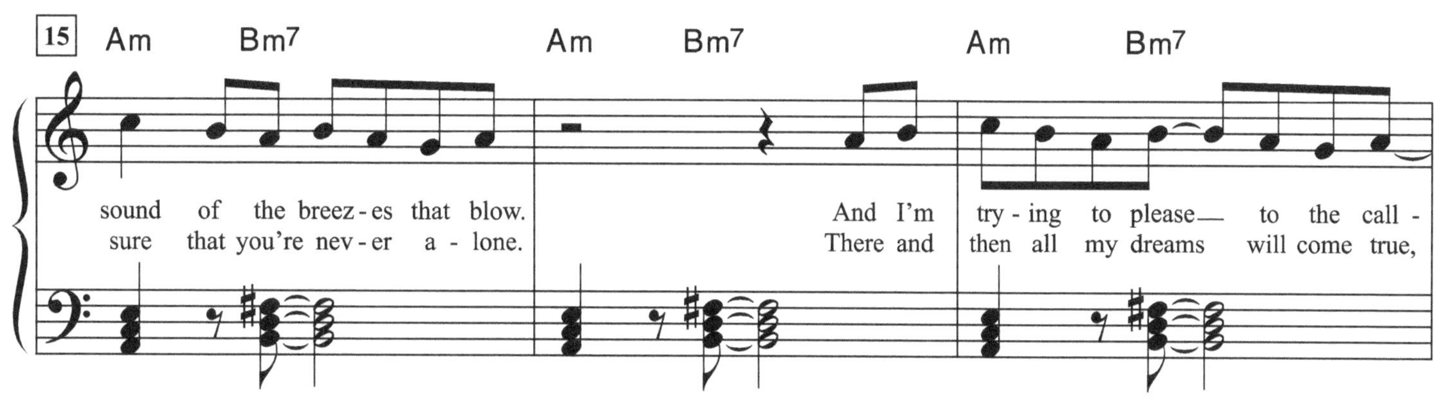
15
Am
Bm7
Am
Bm7
Am
Bm7
sound of the breez - es that blow. And I'm try - ing to please— to the call -
sure that you're nev - er a - lone. There and then all my dreams will come true,

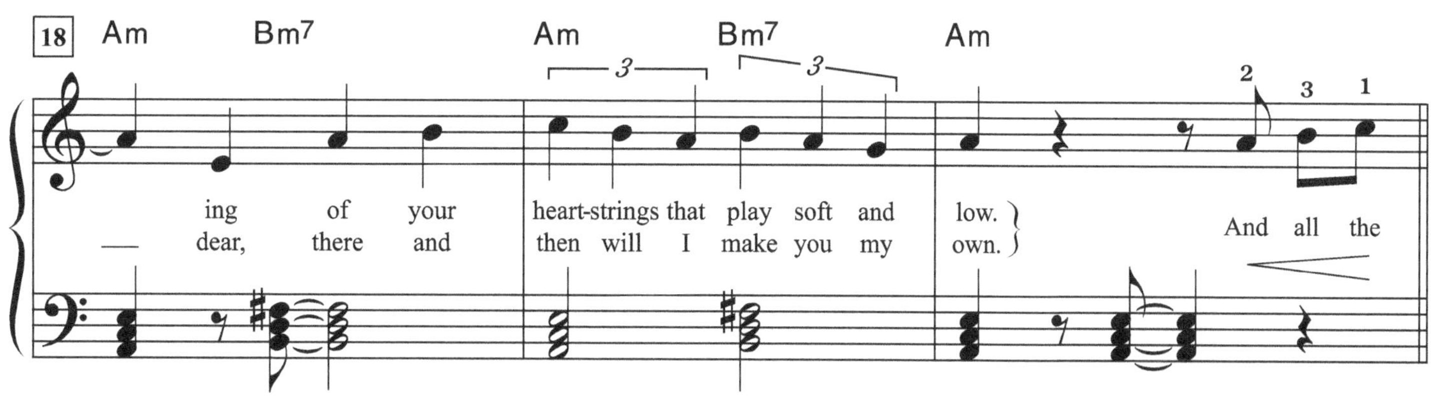
18
Am
Bm7
Am
Bm7
Am
ing of your heart-strings that play soft and low.
— dear, there and then will I make you my own.
And all the

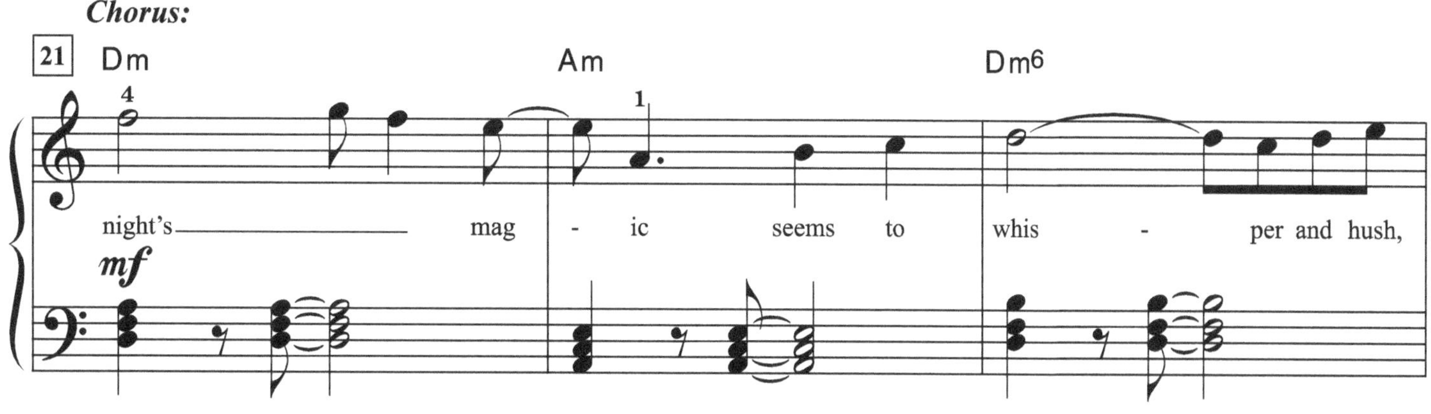
Chorus:
21
Dm
Am
Dm6
night's mag - ic seems to whis - per and hush,
mf

24
Am7
Dm
Am
and all the soft moon - light seems to
27
Dm
E
Am7
Dm
shine in your blush. Can I just have one more
30
Am
Dm
moon - dance with you, my love? Can I
33
Am7
Dm
just make some more ro - mance with you, my
1.
2.
36
Am
E7
love? 2. Well, I
mp
love? One more moon - dance with you
f
Bm

39
Am
Bm
Am
Bm
Am
Bm
in the moon-light on a
42
Am
Bm7
Am7
Bm7
Am7
Bm7
mag - i - cal night.
La la
mf
45
Am7
Bm7
Am7
Bm7
Am7
Bm7
la la, in the moon - light on a
48
Am7
Bm7
Am7
Bm7
Am
Em/G
mag - i - cal night.
Can I just have one
51
Fmaj7
Em7
Dm7
Am9
more moon-dance with you, my love?
rit.
mp

PIECE OF MY HEART

Words and Music by
Jerry Ragovoy and Bert Russell
Arranged by Dan Coates

11
C
E♭
think I've had e - nough, oh, but I'm gon - na show you, ba - by, that a

13
C
wom - an can be tough. I want you to come on, come on, come on, come on and

Chorus:

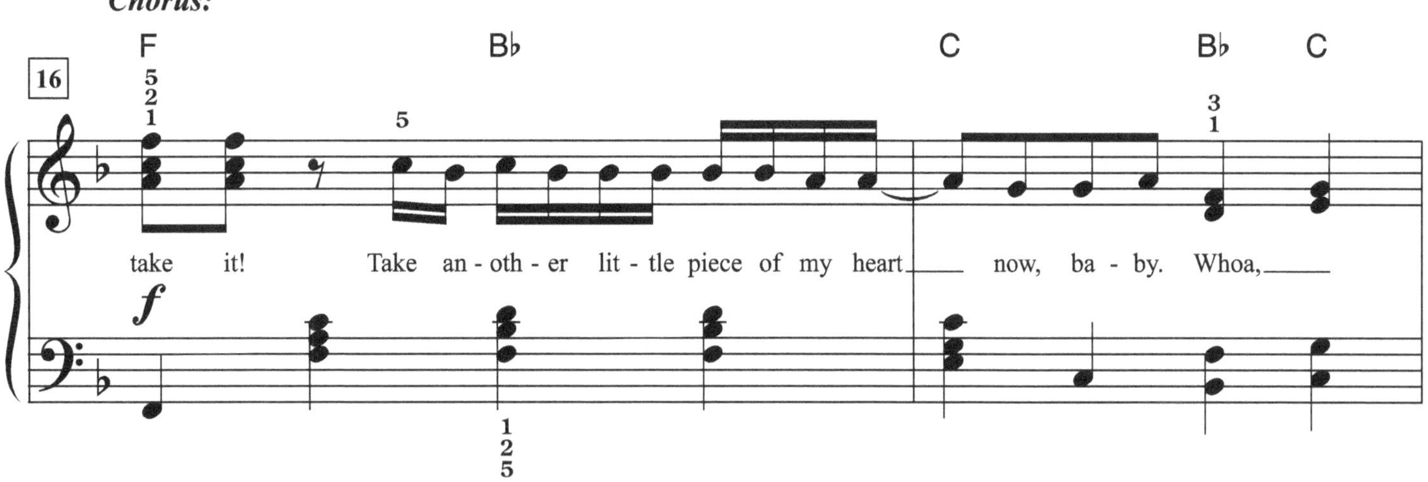
16
F
B♭
C
B♭
C
take it! Take an - oth - er lit - tle piece of my heart now, ba - by. Whoa,

18
F
B♭
C
B♭
C
break it! Break an - oth - er lit - tle bit of my heart. Whoa,

to Coda
20
F
B♭
C
B
have a, have an - oth - er lit - tle piece of my heart now, ba - by.

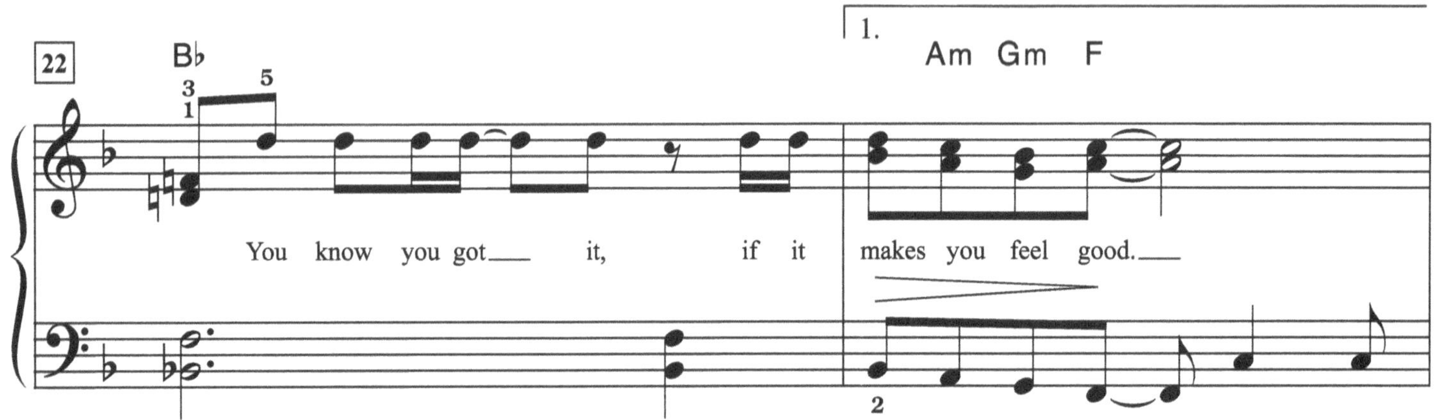
22
B♭
1.
Am Gm F
You know you got it, if it makes you feel good.

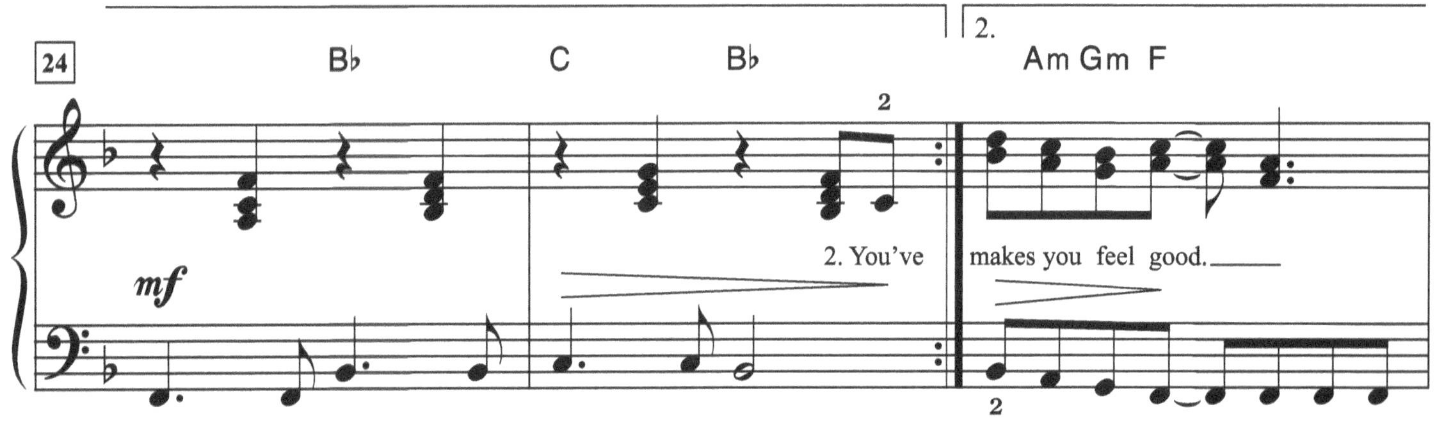
24
B♭
C
B♭
2.
Am Gm F
mf
2. You've
makes you feel good.

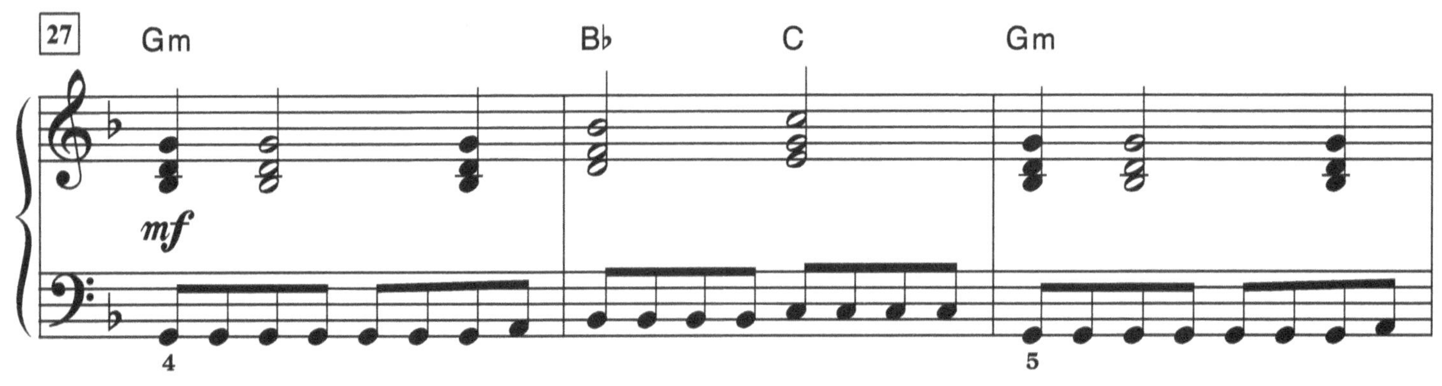
27
Gm
B♭
C
Gm
mf

Verse 2:
You're out on the streets lookin' good,
And, baby, deep down in your heart
I guess you know that it ain't right.
Never, never, never, never, never,
Never hear me when I cry at night,
Baby, I cry all the time.
But each time I tell myself that I,
Well, I can't stand the pain.
But when you hold me in your arms,
I'll sing it once again.
I said come on, come on, come on, come on and...
(To Chorus:)

PINBALL WIZARD

Words and Music by Peter Townshend
Arranged by Dan Coates

Moderate rock
Verse:
C
1. Ev - er since I was a young boy, I played the sil - ver ball. From
mf

B♭
A♭
So-ho down to Bright-on, I must have played 'em all. But I ain't seen noth-in' like him in

G
an - y a-muse-ment hall. That deaf, dumb,_ and blind kid sure plays a mean pin -

C B♭ E♭ F
C B♭ E♭ F
ball.

12
C
2. He
stands like a stat - ue, be-comes part of the ma - chine.
3. Ain't got no dis - trac - tions, can't hear no buzzers and bells. Don't

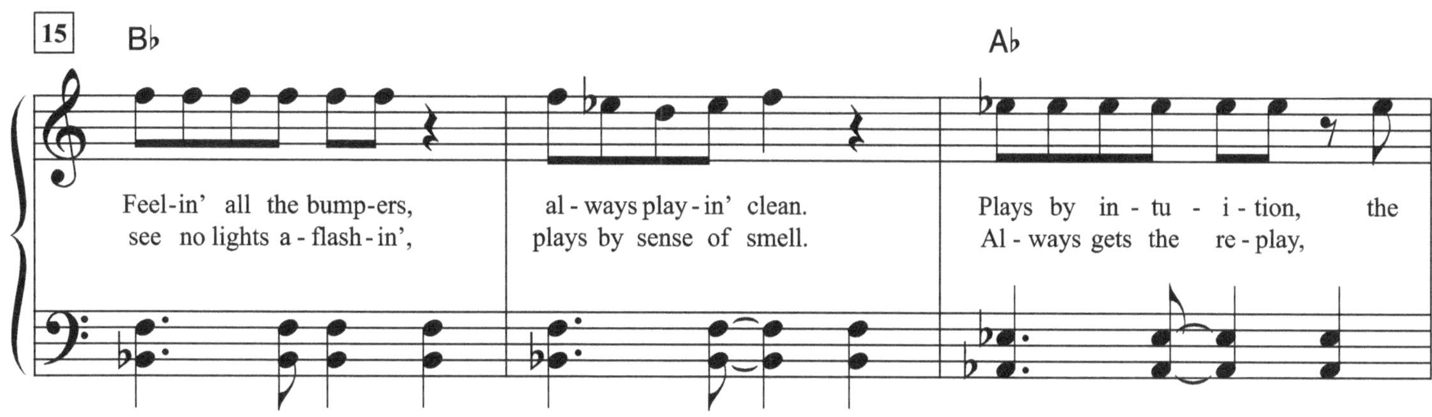
15
B♭
A♭
Feel-in' all the bump-ers, al - ways play - in' clean. Plays by in - tu - i - tion, the
see no lights a - flash - in', plays by sense of smell. Al - ways gets the re - play,

18
G
dig - it count - ers fall. That deaf, dumb, and blind kid sure plays a mean pin -
nev - er seen him fall. That deaf, dumb, and blind kid sure plays a mean pin -

21
C B♭ E♭ F
C B♭ E♭ F
ball.
ball.

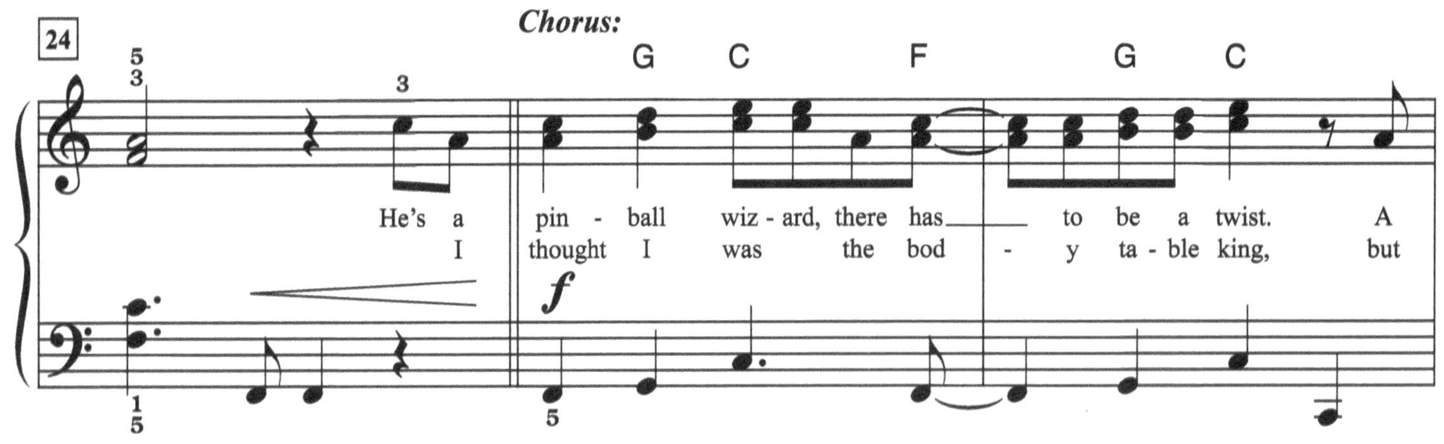
24
Chorus:
G C F G C
He's a pin - ball wiz - ard, there has to be a twist. A
I thought I was the bod - y ta - ble king, but
f

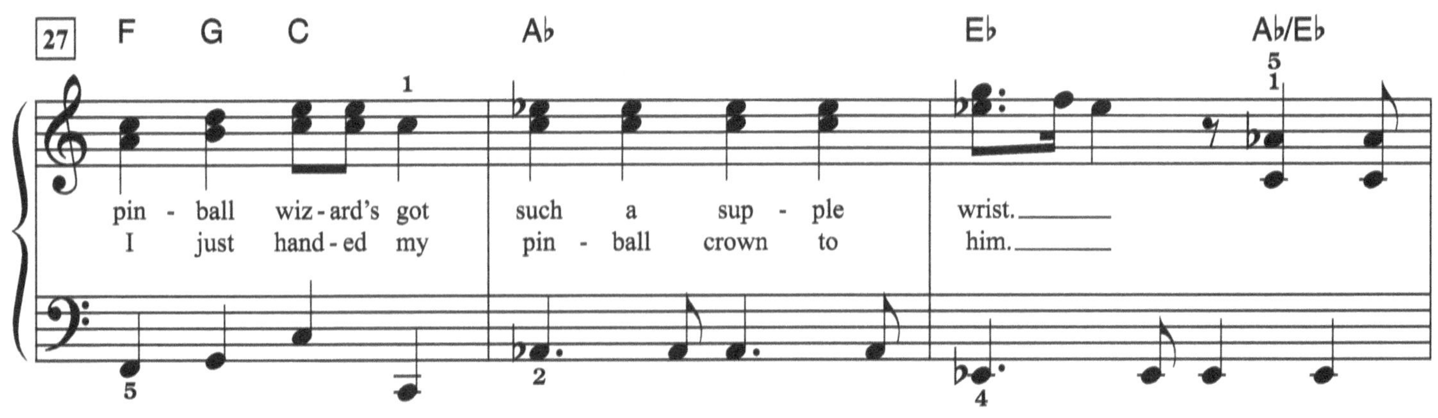
27
F G C
A♭
E♭
A♭/E♭
pin - ball wiz - ard's got such a sup - ple wrist.
I just hand - ed my pin - ball crown to him.

1.
30
E♭
E♭7
D♭
E♭
D♭
How do you think he does it?

33
E♭
A♭
E♭
2.
E♭
What makes him so good?
mf
4. Ev-en

36
Verse:
D♭
on my fav-'rite ta-ble, he can beat my best. His di-sci-ples lead him in, and
mf

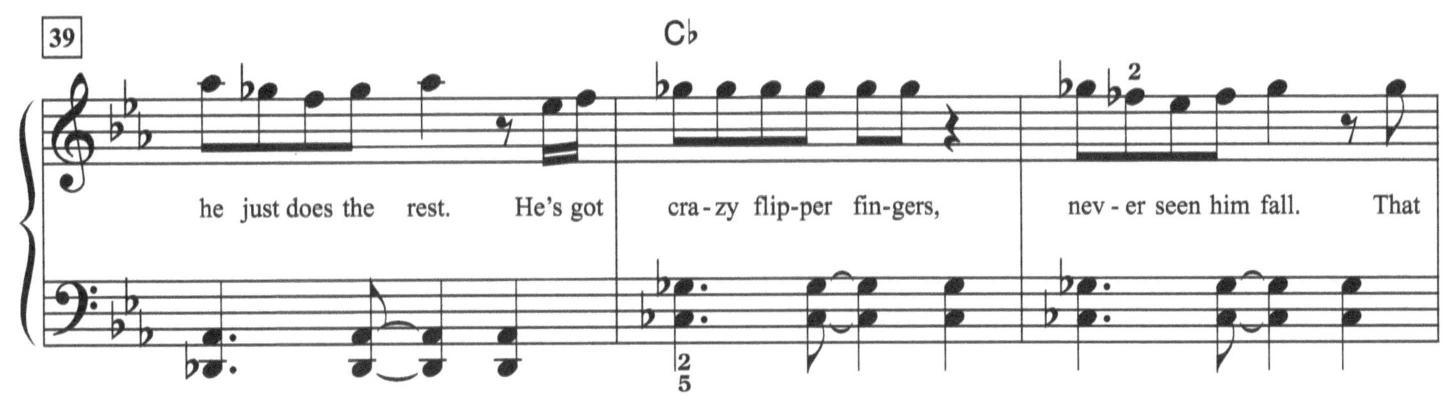
39
C♭
he just does the rest. He's got cra-zy flip-per fin-gers, nev-er seen him fall. That

42
B♭
E♭ D♭ G♭ E♭
deaf, dumb, and blind kid sure plays a mean pin-ball.

45
D♭ G♭ E♭
f

(I CAN'T GET NO) SATISFACTION

Words and Music by
Mick Jagger and Keith Richards
Arranged by Dan Coates

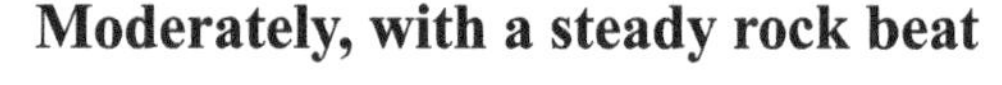

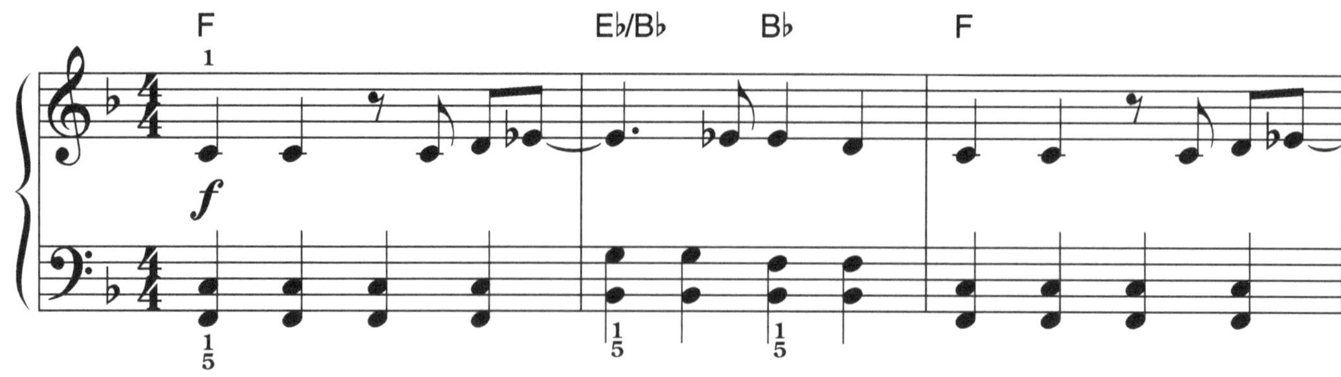

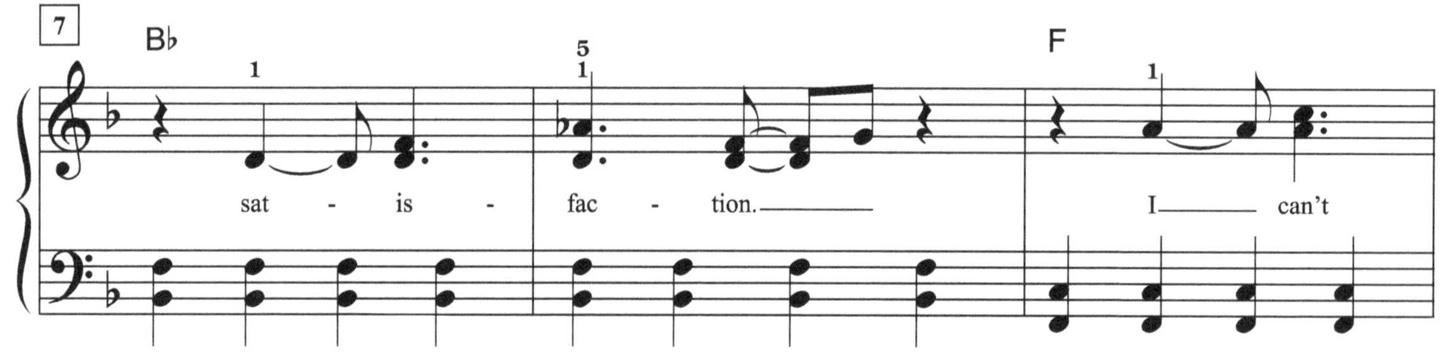

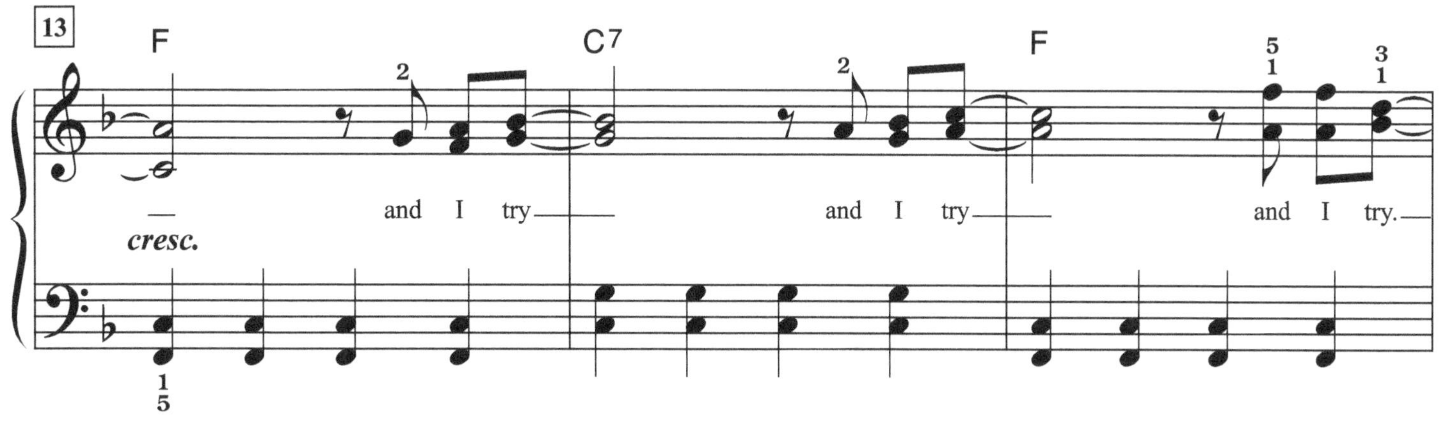
13
F
C7
F
and I try
and I try
and I try.
cresc.

16
B♭
F
E♭/B♭
B♭
I can't
get no,
I can't
f

Verse:
19
F
E♭/B♭
B♭
F
get no...
1. When I'm
2., 3. See additional lyrics.
driv - in' in my car

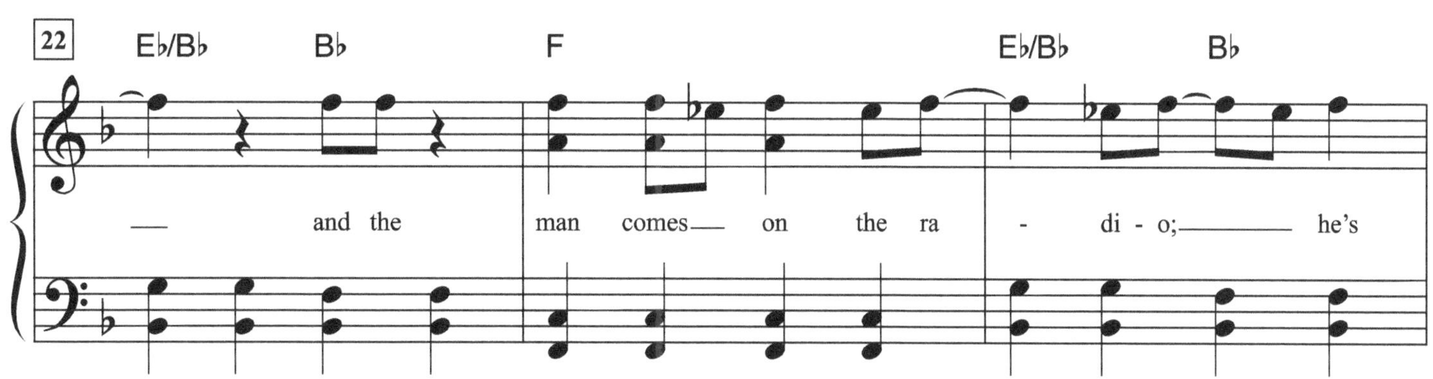
22
E♭/B♭
B♭
F
E♭/B♭
B♭
and the
man comes on the ra - di - o; he's

25
F
Eb/Bb
Bb
F
tell - in' me more and more a - bout some use - less in - for - ma -

28
Eb/Bb
Bb
F
Eb/Bb
Bb
- tion sup - posed to fire my im - ag - i - na - tion. I can't

31
F
Eb/Bb
Bb
F
get no... Oh, no, no, no.

34
F
Eb/Bb
Bb
Hey, hey, hey. That's what I say.

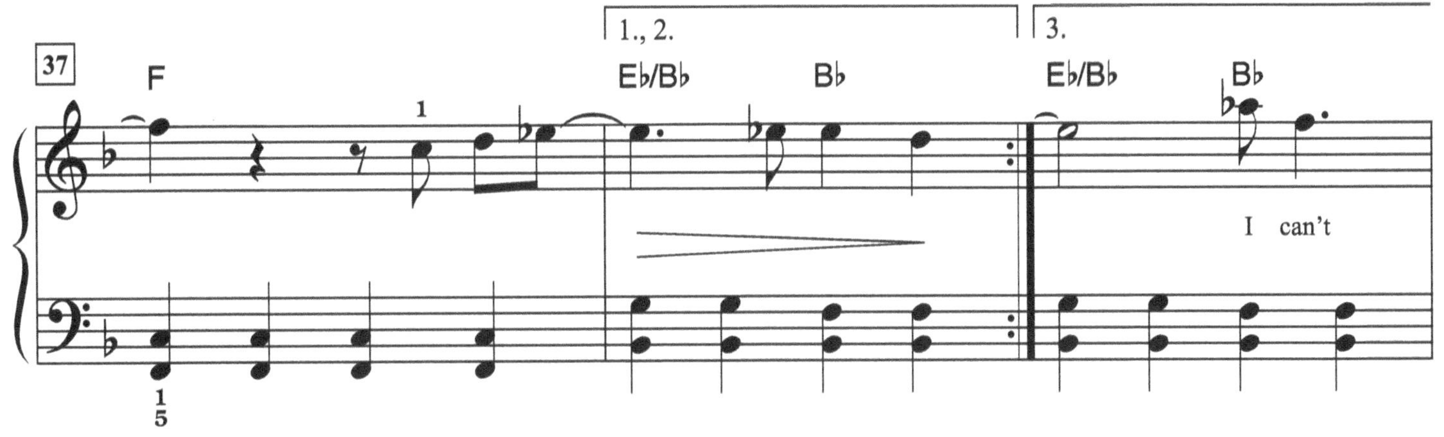

Verse 2:
When I'm watchin' my T.V.
And a man comes on and tells me
How white my shirts can be.
But, he can't be a man
'Cause he doesn't smoke the same cigarettes as me.
I can't get no,
Oh, no, no, no.

Verse 3:
When I'm ridin' 'round the world,
And I'm doin' this and I'm signin' that,
And I'm tryin' to make some girl,
Who tells me, baby, better come back maybe next week.
'Cause you see I'm on a losin' streak.
I can't get no,
Oh, no, no, no.

STAIRWAY TO HEAVEN

Words and Music by
Jimmy Page and Robert Plant
Arranged by Dan Coates

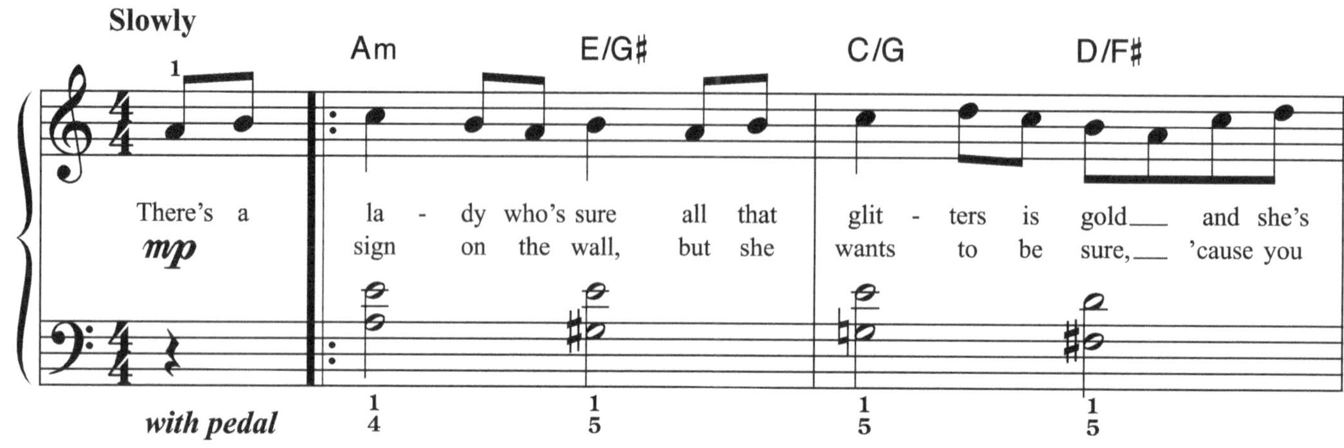

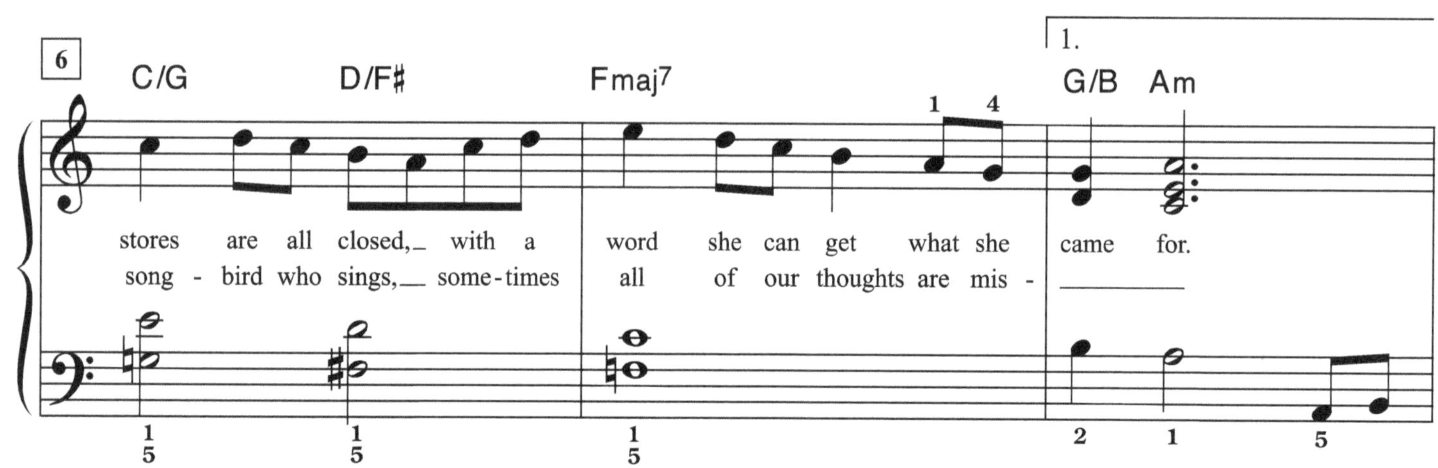

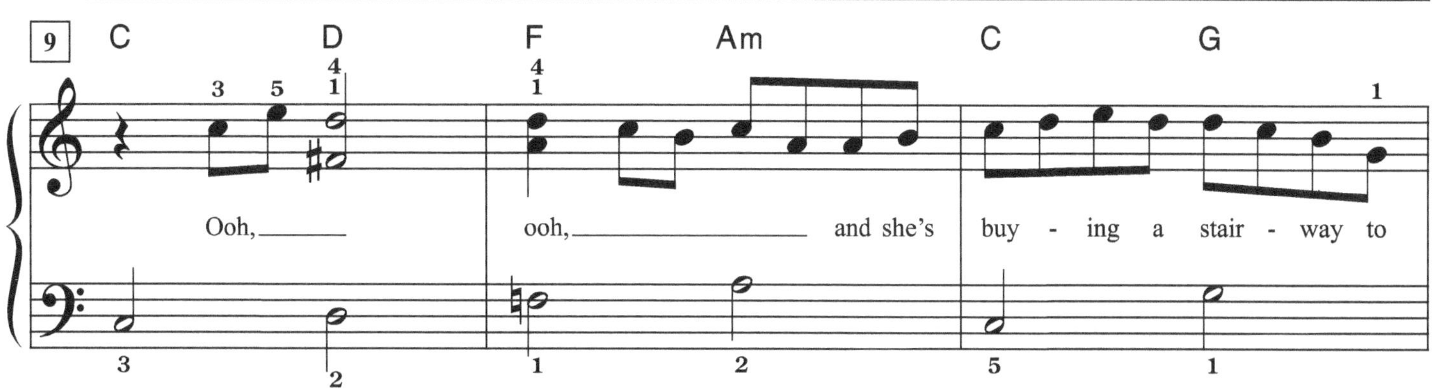
9
C
D
F
Am
C
G
Ooh,
ooh,
and she's
buy - ing a stair - way to

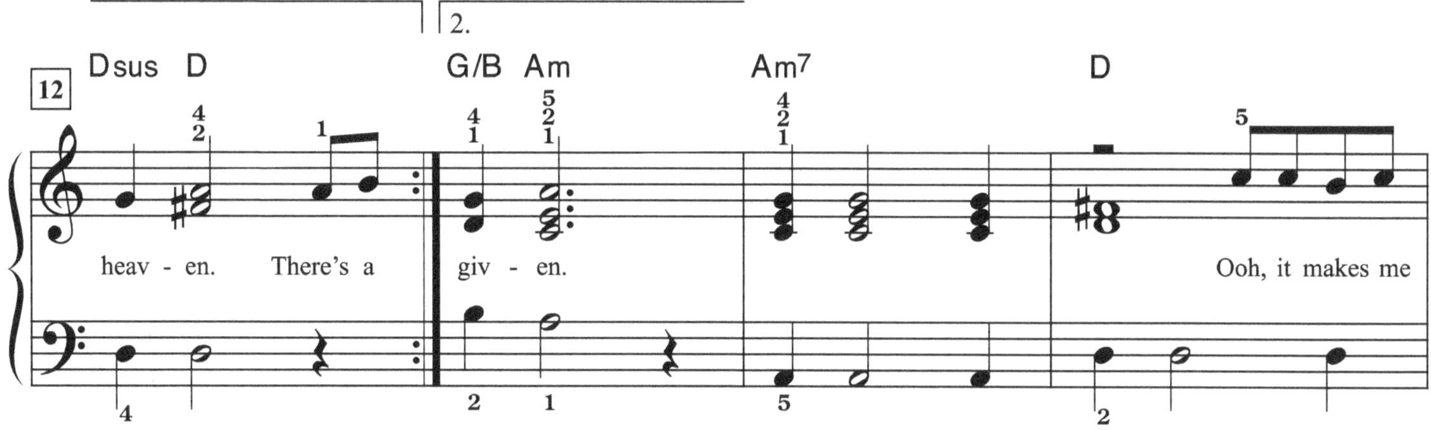
12
2.
Dsus D
G/B Am
Am7
D
heav - en. There's a
giv - en.
Ooh, it makes me

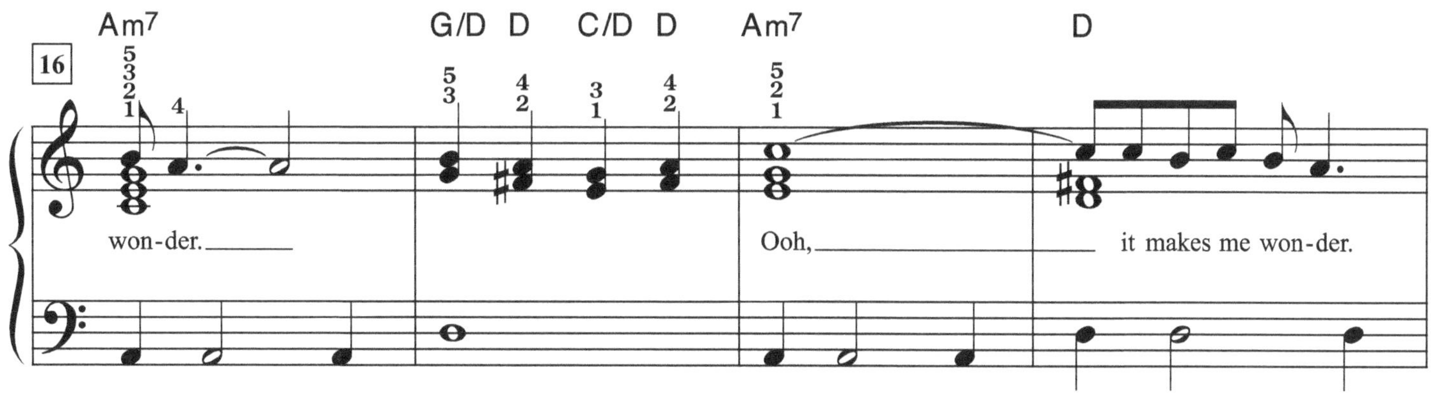
16
Am7
G/D D C/D D
Am7
D
won-der.
Ooh,
it makes me won-der.

20
Am7
G/D D C/D
C G/B
There's a
mf
feel - ing I get when I
whis - pered that soon if we

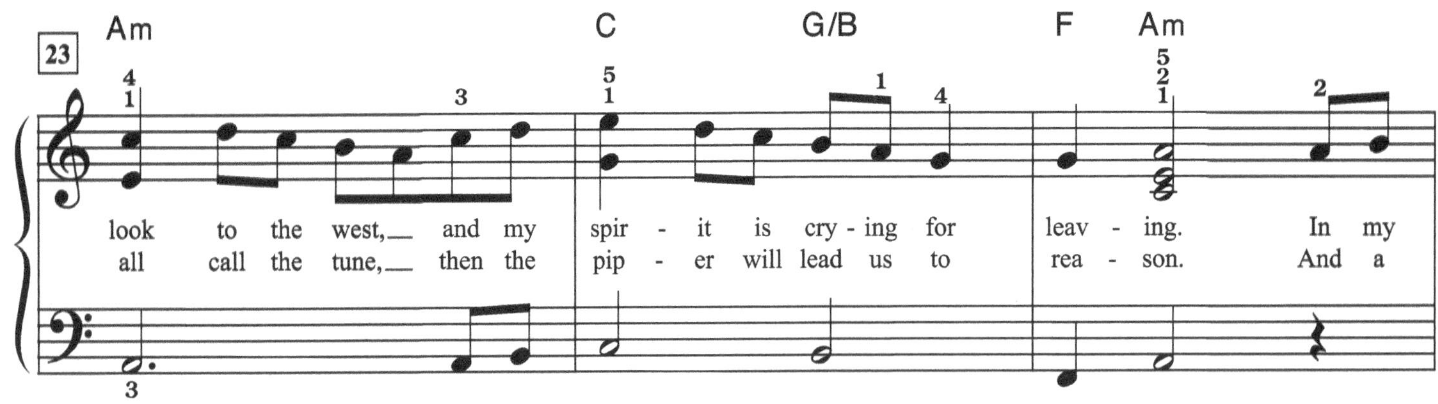
23
Am
C
G/B
F
Am
look to the west, and my spir - it is cry - ing for leav - ing. In my
all call the tune, then the pip - er will lead us to rea - son. And a

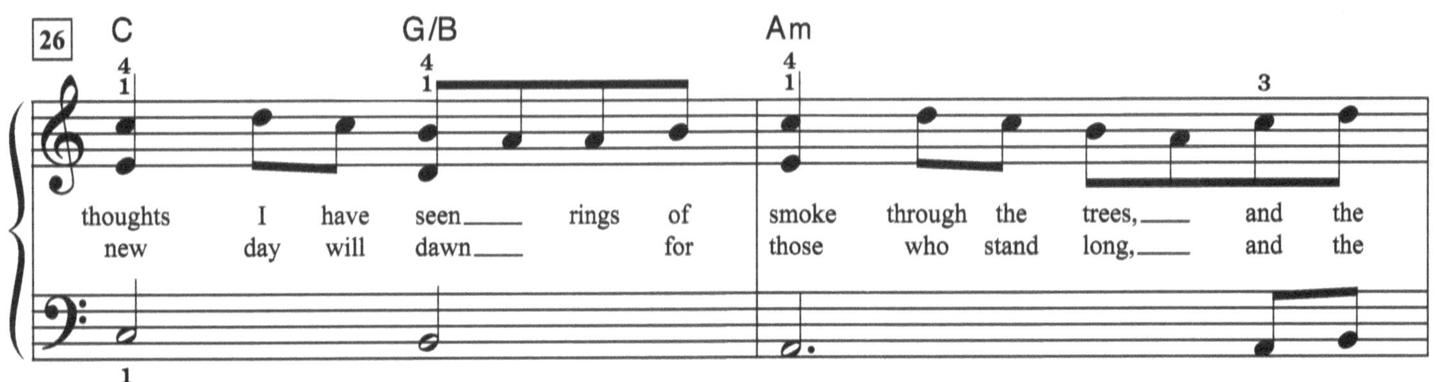
26
C
G/B
Am
thoughts I have seen rings of smoke through the trees, and the
new day will dawn for those who stand long, and the

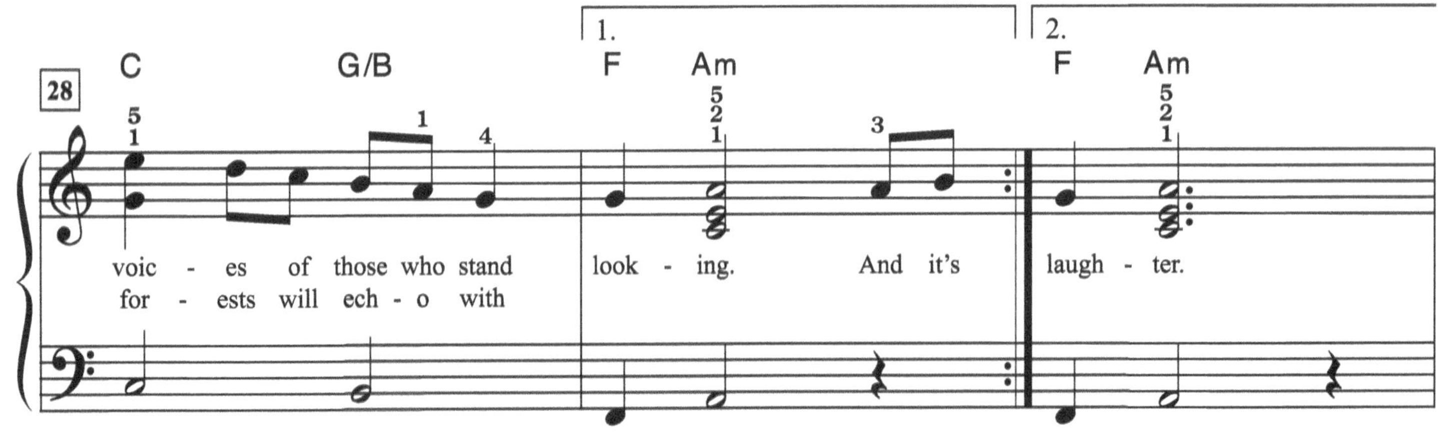
1.
2.
28
C
G/B
F
Am
F
Am
voic - es of those who stand look - ing. And it's laugh - ter.
for - ests will ech - o with

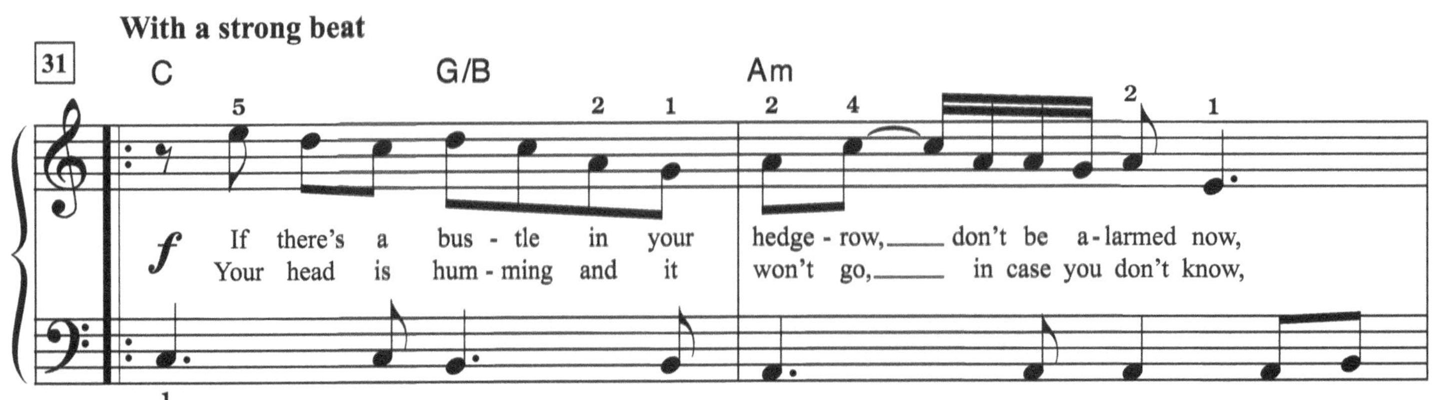
With a strong beat
31
C
G/B
Am
f
If there's a bus - tle in your hedge - row, don't be a - larmed now,
Your head is hum - ming and it won't go, in case you don't know,

33
C G/B F Am
it's just a spring clean for the May queen.
the pip - er's call - ing you to join him.

35
C G/B Am
Yes, there are two paths you can go by, but in the long run,
Dear la - dy, can you hear the wind blow, and did you know

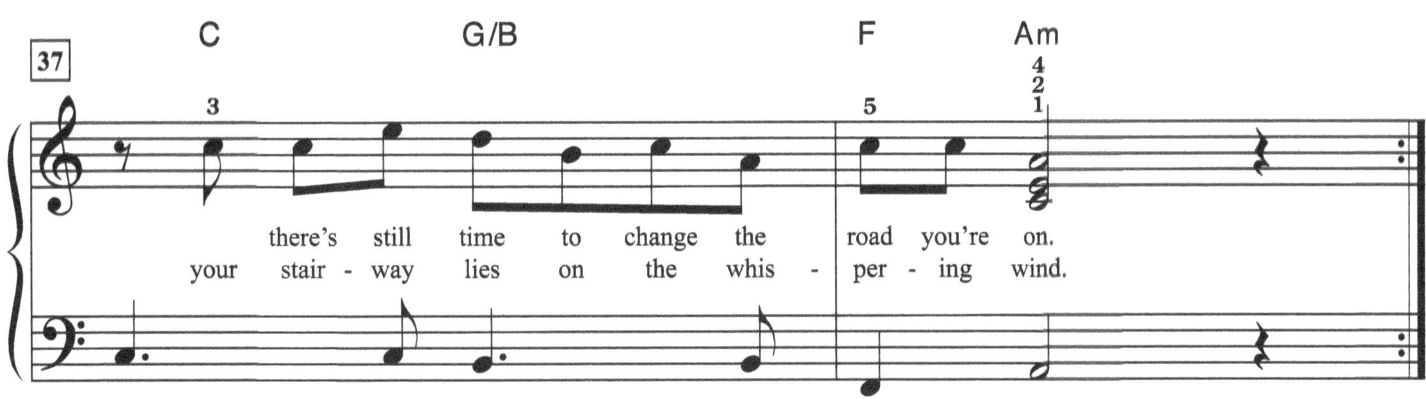
37
C G/B F Am
there's still time to change the road you're on.
your stair - way lies on the whis - per - ing wind.

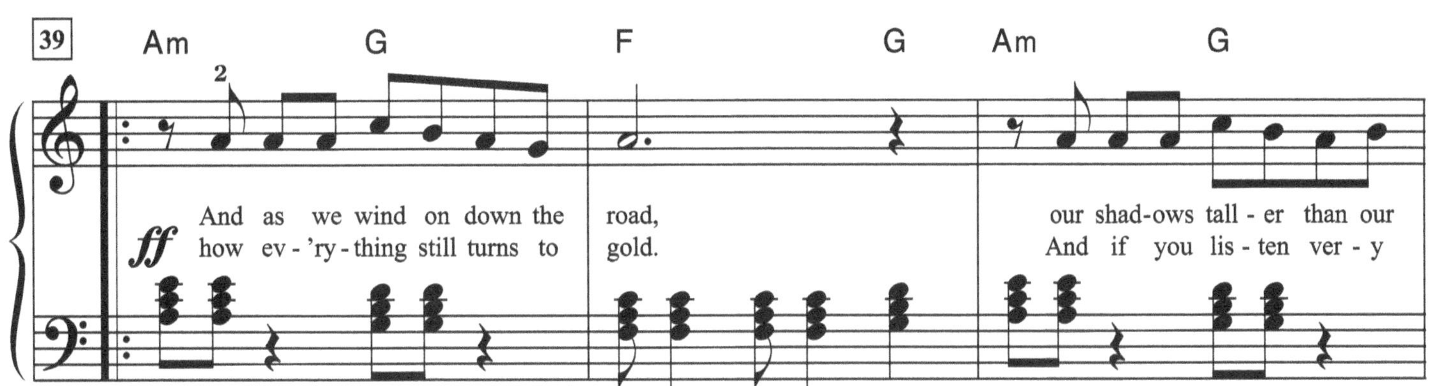
39
Am G F G Am G
And as we wind on down the road, our shad-ows tall - er than our
how ev - 'ry - thing still turns to gold. And if you lis - ten ver - y
ff

42
F G Am G F G
soul.
hard,
There walks a la - dy we all know,
the tune will come to you at last,

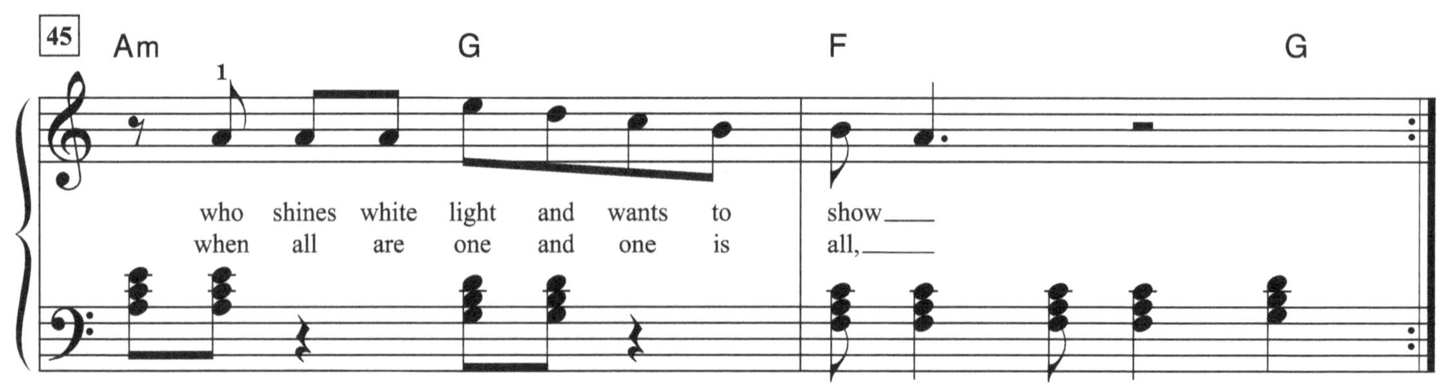
45
Am G F G
who shines white light and wants to show
when all are one and one is all,

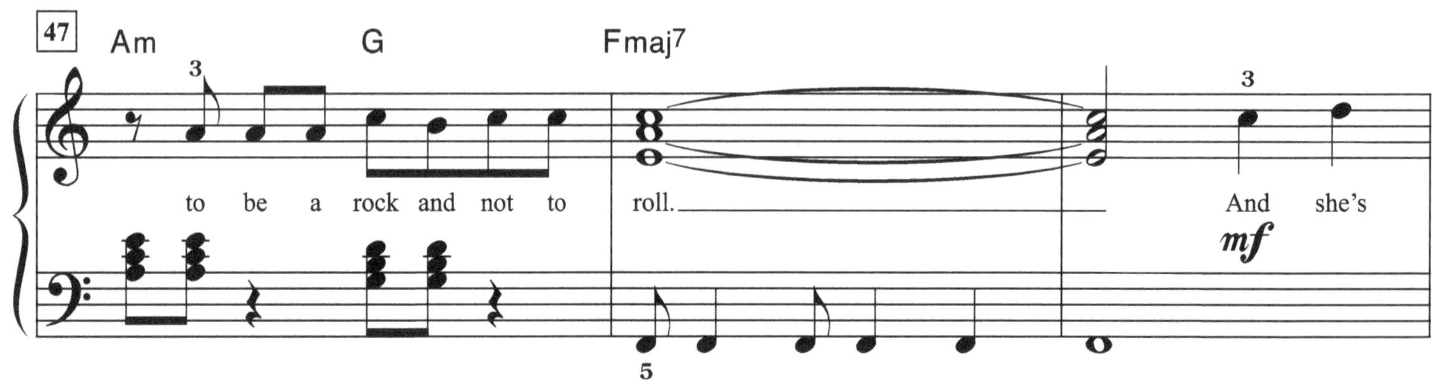
47
Am G Fmaj7
to be a rock and not to roll.
And she's
mf

50
Am
buy - ing a stair - way to heav - en.

THUNDER ROAD

Words and Music by Bruce Springsteen
Arranged by Dan Coates

14
C7/E
F
B♭/F
lone - ly. Hey, that's me, and I want you on - ly. Don't turn me
17
C7/E
home a - gain. I just can't face my - self a - lone a - gain.
20
F
B♭/F
Don't run back in - side, dar - ling, you know just what I'm
23
F
here for. So you're scared and you're think - ing that
26
C/E
B♭/F
may - be we ain't that young an - y - more. Show a lit - tle

29
C7/E
F
C7/G
F/A
faith, there's mag - ic in the
night.
You ain't a
beau - ty, but hey, you're al -
32
B♭
F/A
Gm
F
right.
Oh, and
that's al - right
with
35
C
C7
F
me.
2. You can
mf
hide 'neath your cov - ers and
38
Dm
F
B♭/F
stud - y your pain,
make
cross - es from your lov - ers, throw
ros - es in the rain,
41
F
Am/E
B♭/F
waste your sum - mer
pray - ing in vain
for a
sav - ior to rise
from these

44
C7sus
C7
F
Dm
streets. Well now, I'm no he - ro, that's un - der - stood. All the re -
47
F
B♭/F
C7
F
demp - tion I can of - fer, girl, is be - neath this dir - ty hood, with a chance to make it
50
Dm
B♭/D
C7
good some - how. Hey, what else can we do now, ex - cept
53
F
B♭/F
F
roll down the win - dow and let the wind blow back your hair.
56
Am/E
Well, the night's bust - ing o - pen, these two lanes will take us

59
B♭/F
an - y - where. We got one last chance to make it
62
C7/E
F
B♭/F
real, to trade in these wings on some wheels.
65
F
C7
Climb in back, heav - en's wait - ing down on the tracks.
Chorus:
69
F
Dm
F
mf
Oh, come take my hand, rid - ing out to - night to
72
B♭/F
F
Am/E
case the prom - ised land. Oh, Thun - der Road,

75
B♭/F
C7/E
F
oh, Thun - der Road,
oh, Thun - der Road.
Ly - ing out there like a
78
Dm
F
B♭/F
kill - er in the sun.
Hey, I know it's late, we can
make it if we run.
81
F
Am/E
B♭/F
Oh,
Thun - der Road, sit
tight,
take
84
C7/E
F
hold,
Thun - der
Road.
Well, I
Bridge:
87
B♭/F
C7/E
F
got this gui - tar, and I
learned how to make it talk.

90
Dm
Bb/D
5
And my car's out back, if you're read - y to take that long
1
3
5
94
C/E
Bb/F
C/E
2
walk from your front porch to my front seat. The door's
97
Am/E
Dm
Bb
Dm/A
1
o - pen but the ride ain't free, and I know you're lone-ly for words that
100
Gm7
C7
4
I ain't spo - ken, but to - night we'll be free. All the prom - is - es will be bro - ken. There were
103
F
Bb/F
F
5
ghosts in the eyes of all the boys you sent a - way.

106
Am/E
They haunt this dust - y beach road in the skel - e - ton frames of
109
B♭/F
burned out Chev - ro - lets. They scream your name at night in the
112
C/E
F
B♭/F
street, your grad - u - a - tion gown lies in rags at their feet. And in the
115
Am/E
B♭/F
lone - ly cool be - fore dawn, you hear their en - gines roar - ing
118
Gm
C
on. But when you get to the porch, they're gone on the

121
B♭/F
Gm
wind.
So, Mar - y, climb
in.
It's a
125
B♭/F
C7
F
town full of los-ers. I'm
pull-ing out of here to win.
129
F
C
F
132
B♭
F
C
135
B♭
C
F

A WHITER SHADE OF PALE

Words and Music by
Keith Reid and Gary Brooker
Arranged by Dan Coates

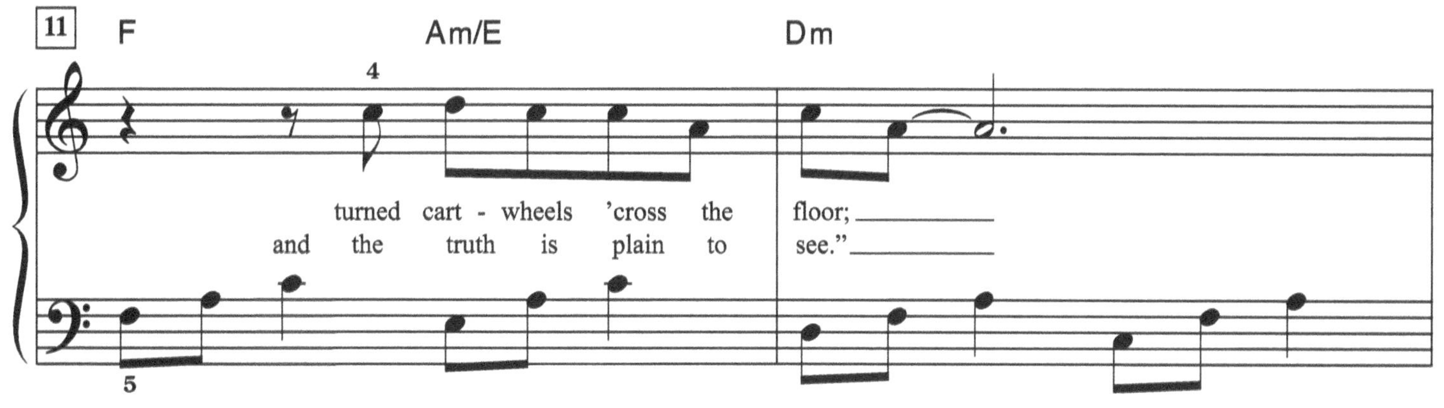
11
F
Am/E
Dm
turned cart - wheels 'cross the floor;
and the truth is plain to see."

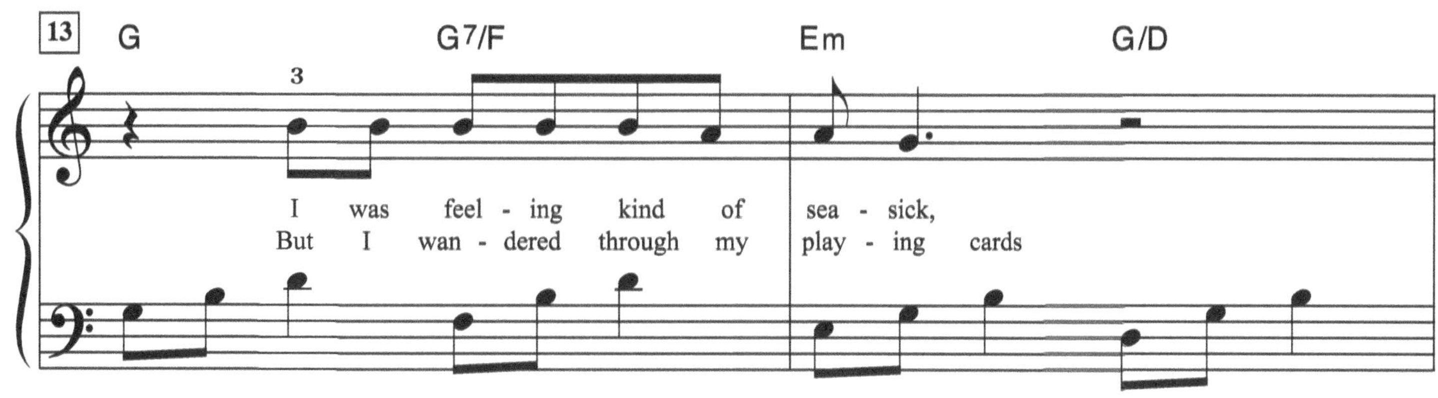
13
G
G7/F
Em
G/D
I was feel - ing kind of sea - sick,
But I wan - dered through my play - ing cards

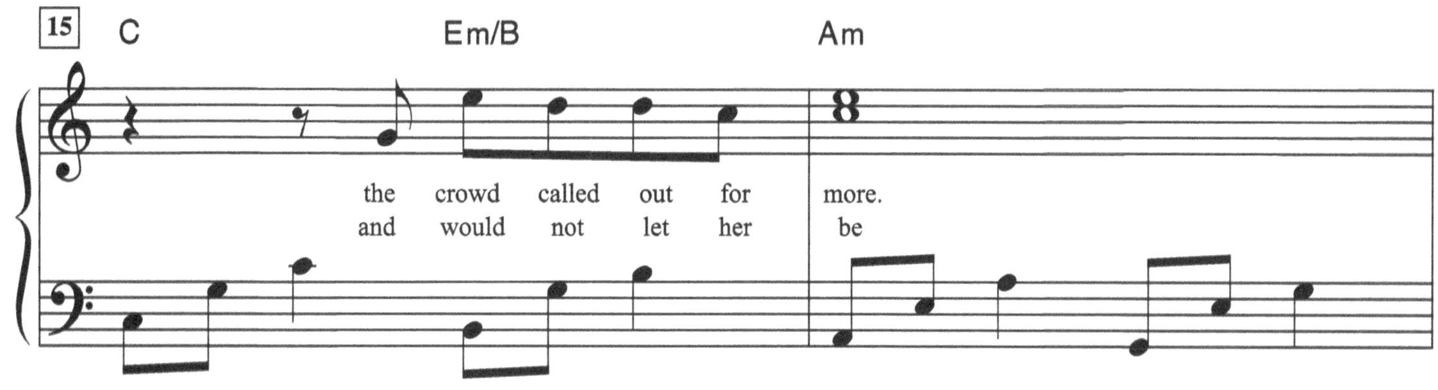
15
C
Em/B
Am
the crowd called out for more.
and would not let her be

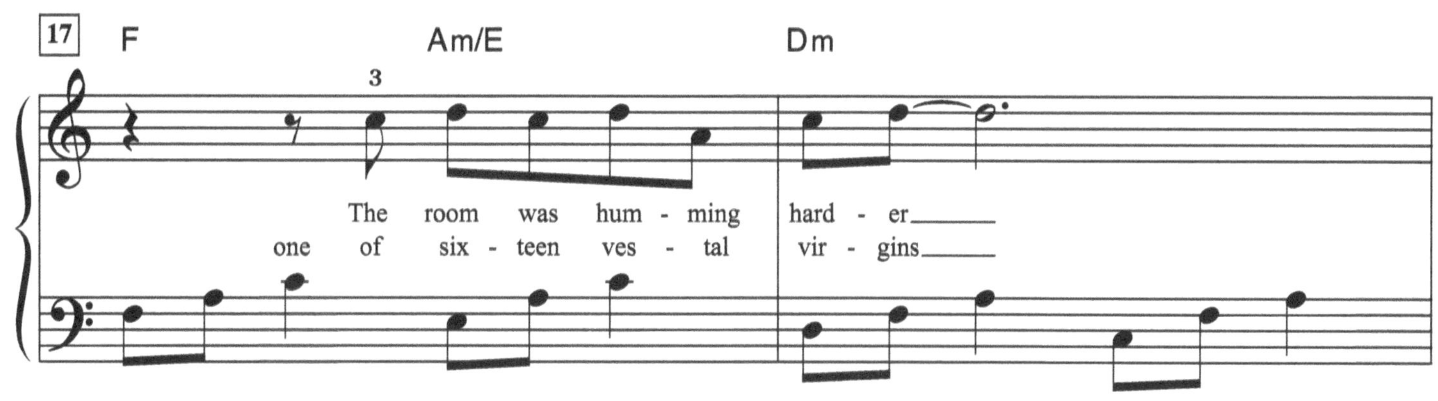
17
F
Am/E
Dm
The room was hum - ming hard - er
one of six - teen ves - tal vir - gins

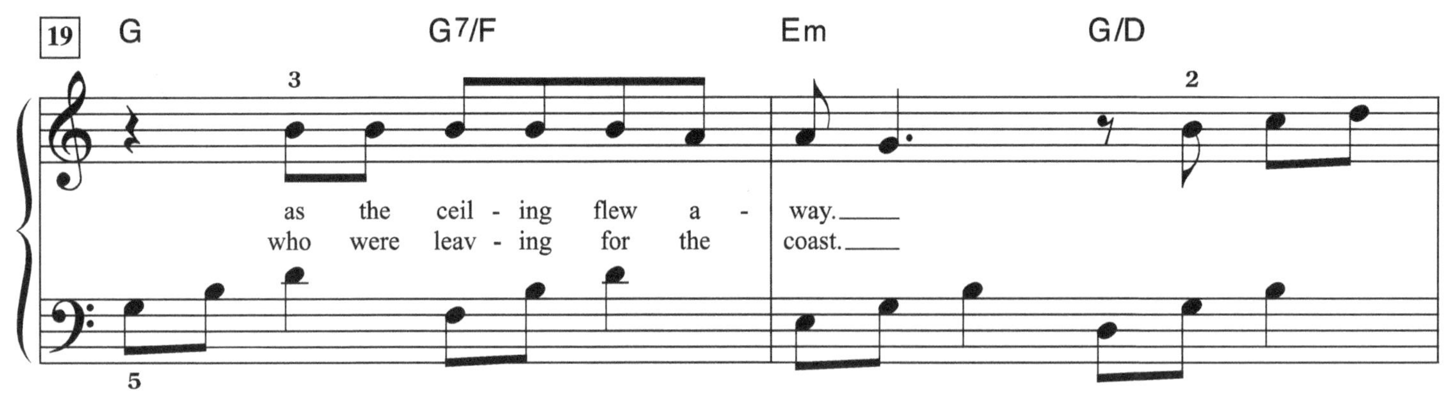
19
G G7/F Em G/D
as the ceil - ing flew a - way.
who were leav - ing for the coast.

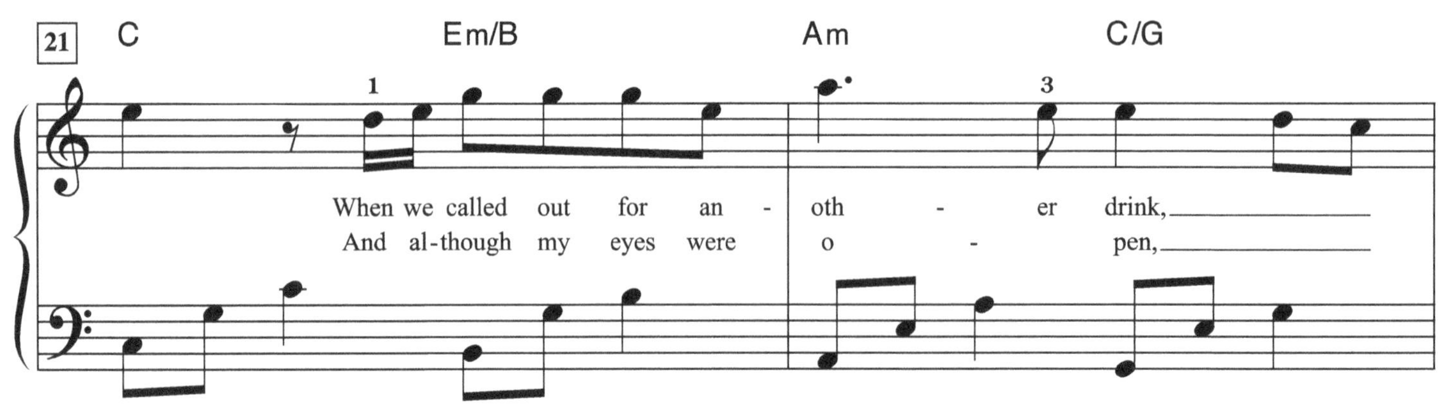
21
C Em/B Am C/G
When we called out for an - oth - er drink,
And al-though my eyes were o - pen,

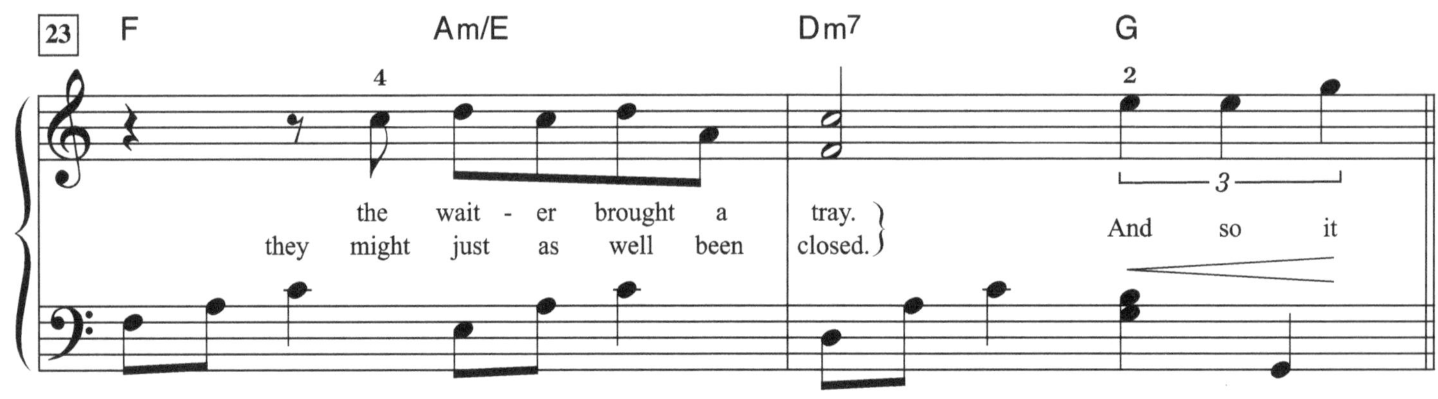
23
F Am/E Dm7 G
the wait - er brought a tray.
they might just as well been closed.
And so it

Chorus:

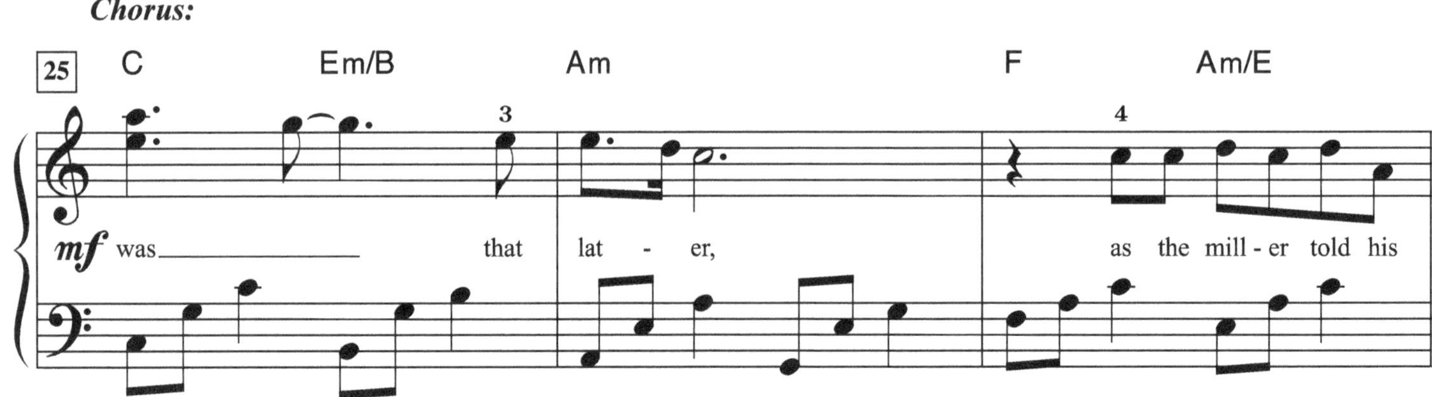
25
C Em/B Am F Am/E
mf
was that lat - er, as the mill - er told his

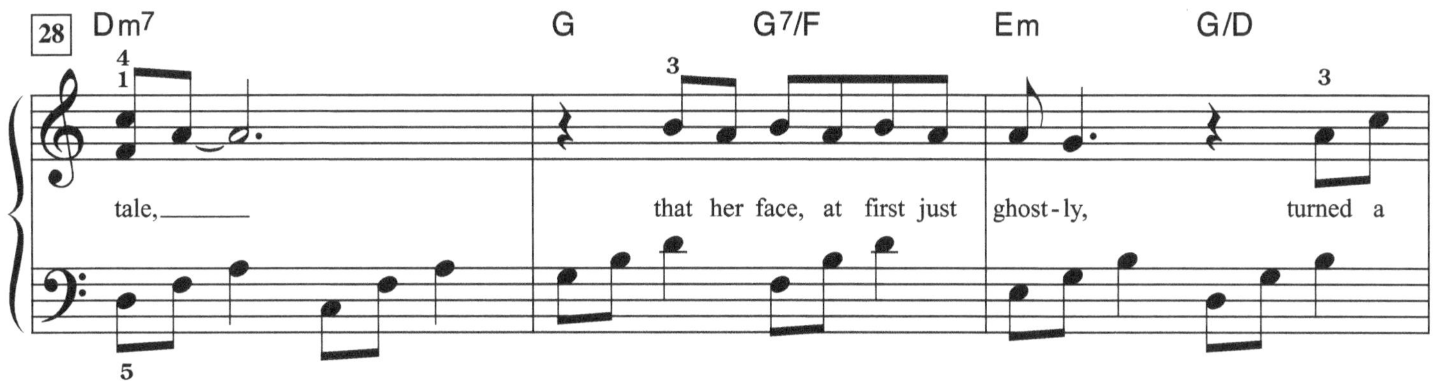
28
Dm7
G
G7/F
Em
G/D
tale,
that her face, at first just
ghost-ly,
turned a

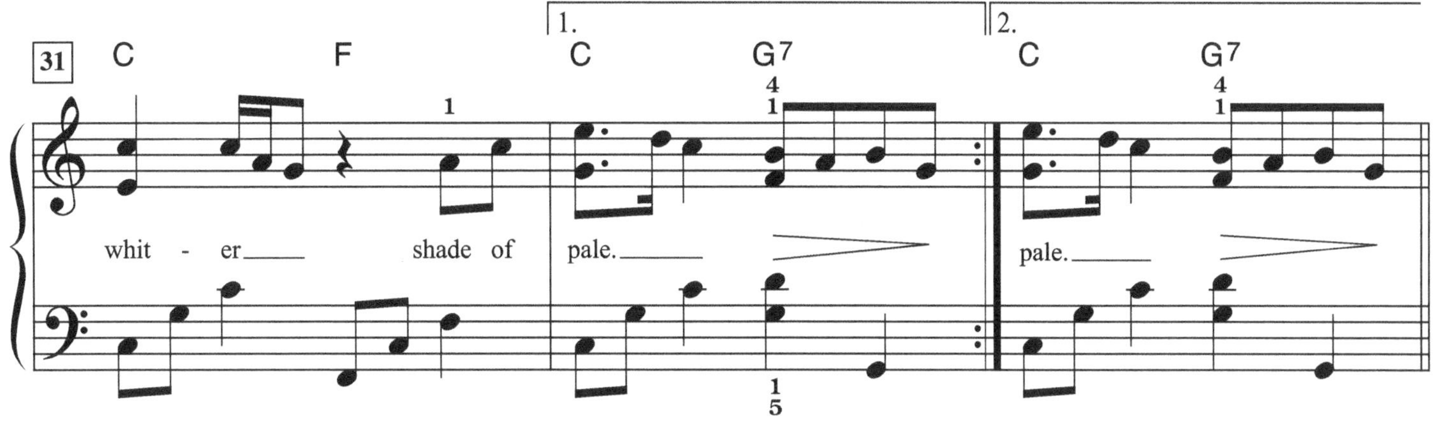
31
C
F
1.
C
G7
2.
C
G7
whit - er
shade of
pale.
pale.

Instrumental:

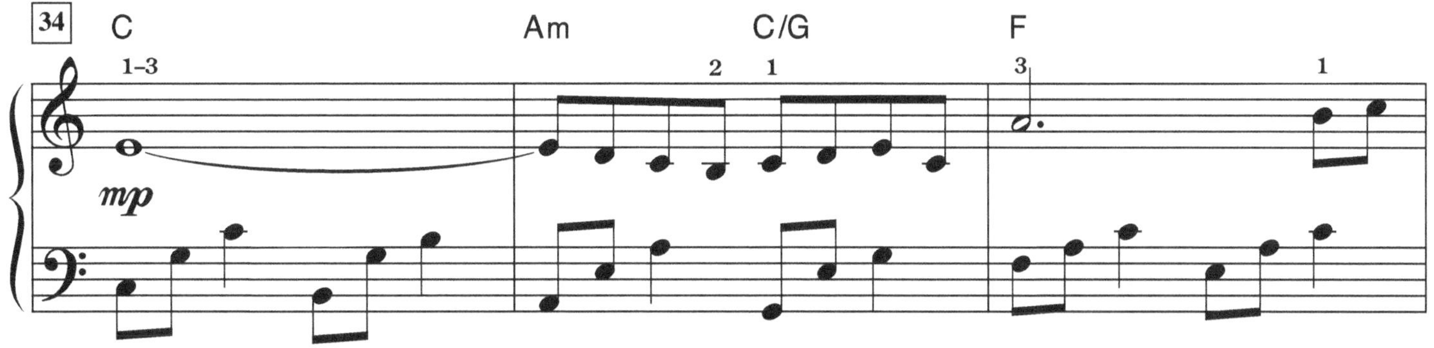
34
C
Am
C/G
F
mp

37
Dm
F/C
G
Em
G/D
cresc.

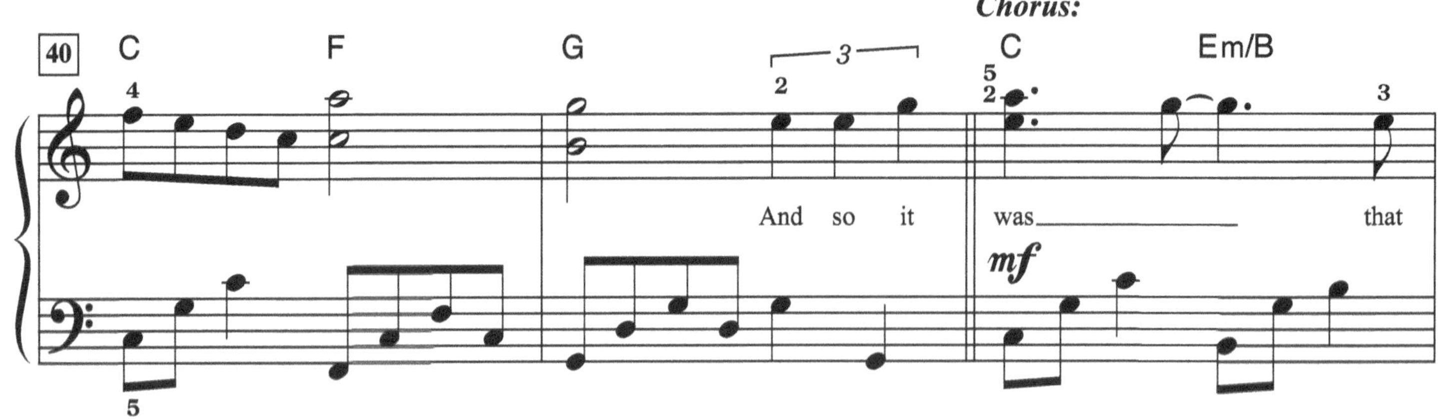
40
C
F
G
Chorus:
C
Em/B
And so it
was
that
mf

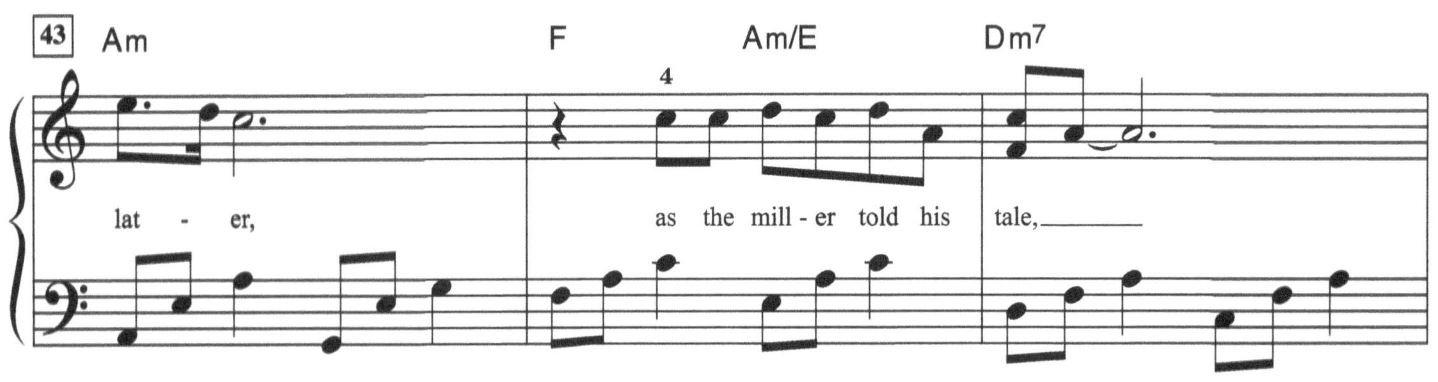
43
Am
F
Am/E
Dm7
lat - er,
as the mill - er told his
tale,

46
G
G7/F
Em
G/D
that her face, at first just
ghost - ly,
turned a

48
C
F
C
G7
C
whit - er
shade of
pale.
rit. e dim.
p

WISH YOU WERE HERE

Words and Music by
Roger Waters and David Gilmour
Arranged by Dan Coates

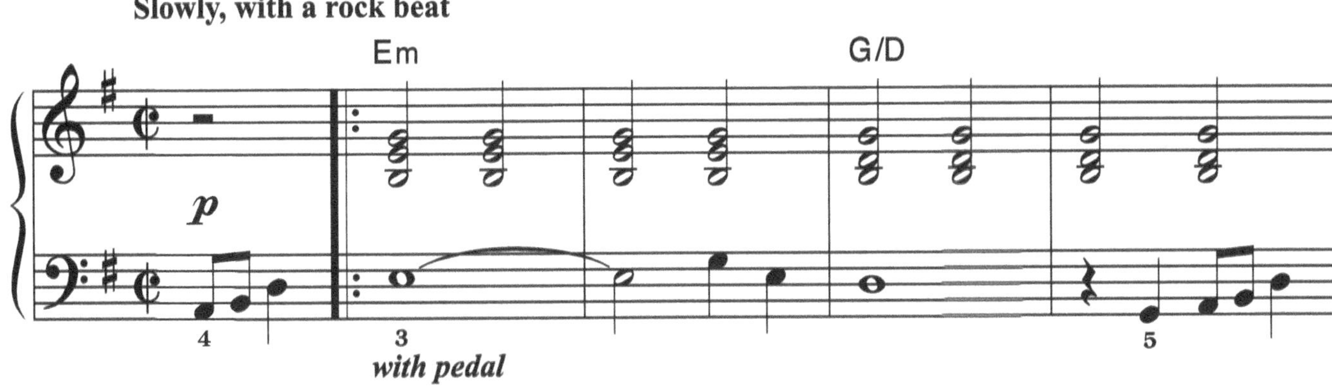

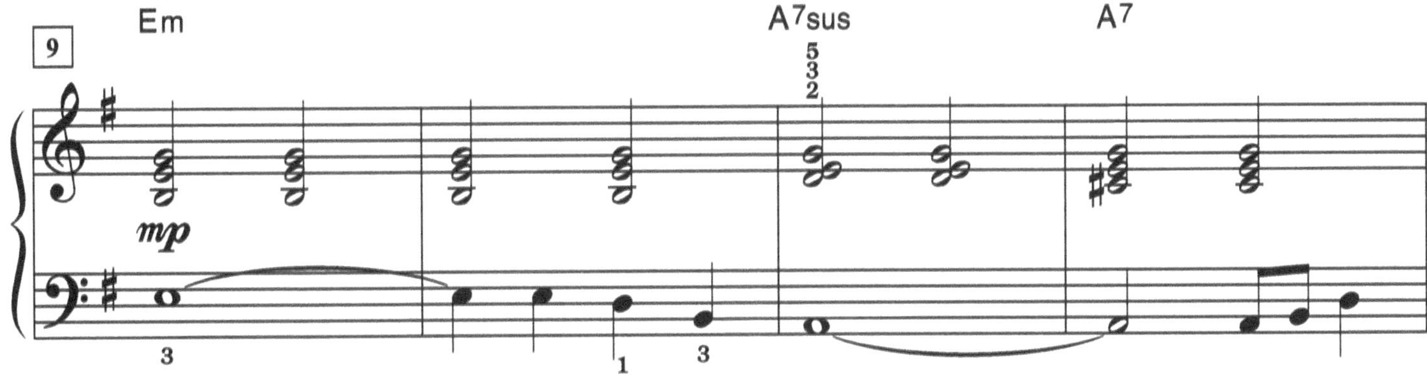

2.
Verse:
17
G
C
mf
So,
so you think you can tell

21
D
Am
heav - en from hell,
blue skies from pain.

25
G
D/F#
Can you tell a green field
from a cold steel

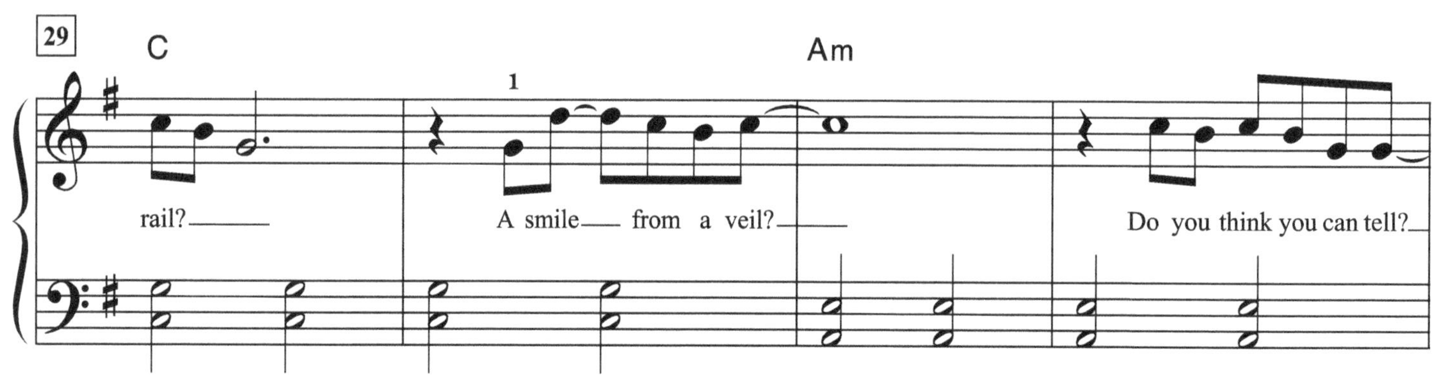
29
C
Am
rail?
A smile from a veil?
Do you think you can tell?

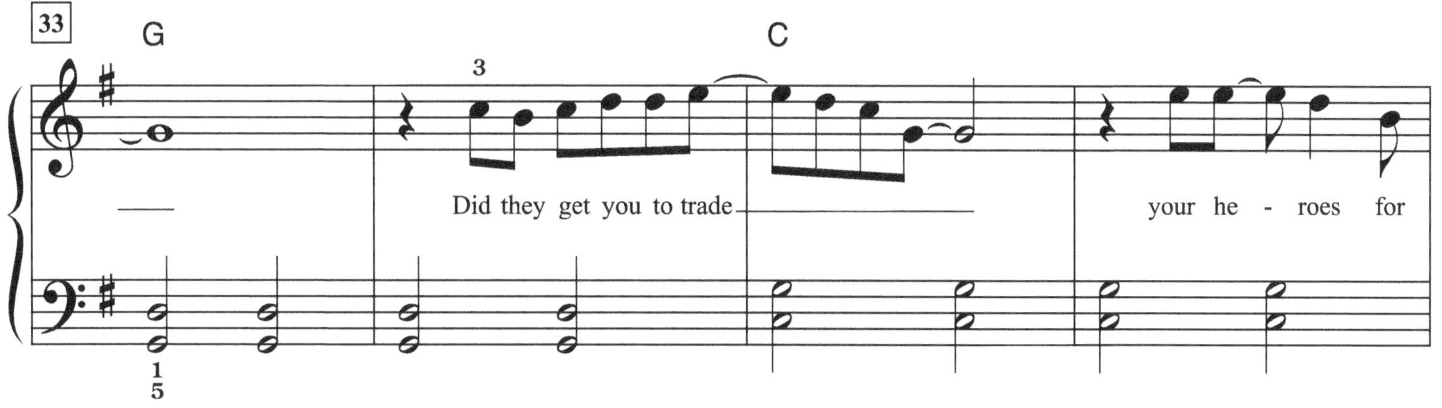
33
G
C
3
Did they get you to trade
your he - roes for
1
5

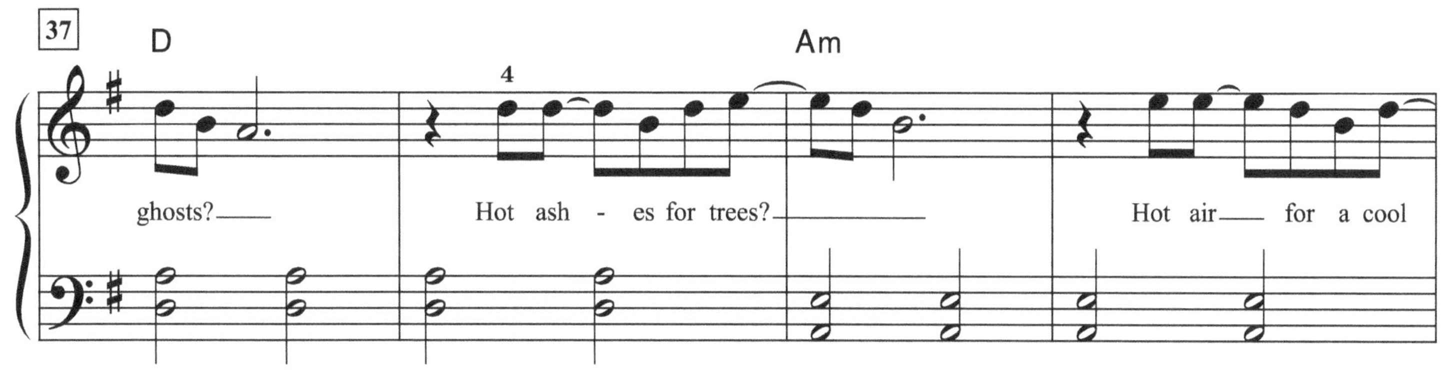
37
D
Am
4
ghosts?
Hot ash - es for trees?
Hot air for a cool

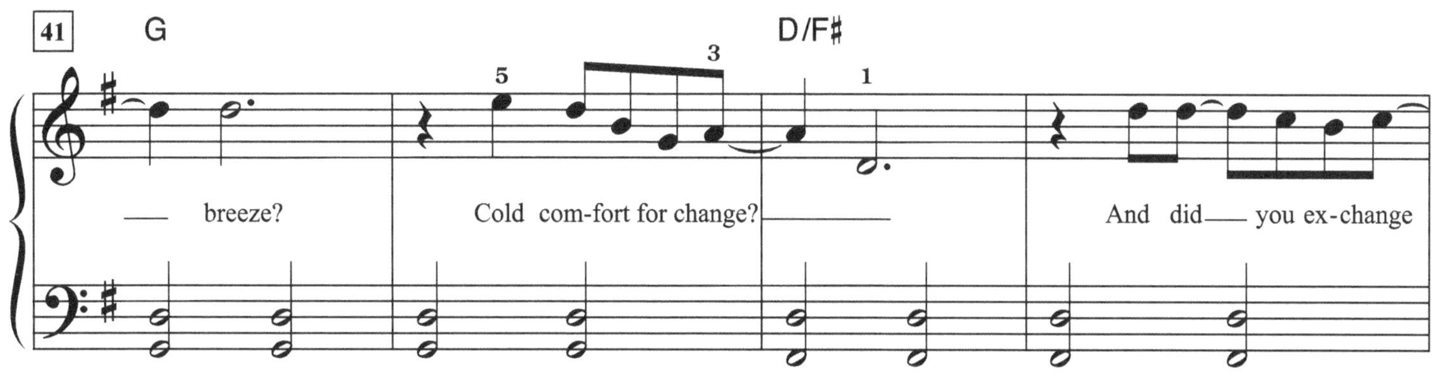
41
G
D/F♯
5
3
1
breeze?
Cold com-fort for change?
And did you ex-change

45
C
Am
1
1
2
a
walk - on part in the war
for a lead role in a cage?

49
G
5
3
1
Em
mp
5
3
53
G/D
Em
5
3
57
G/D
Em
3
1
61
A7sus
A7
Em
3
1
65
A7sus
A7
G
cresc.

Chorus:
69
C
D
f
How I wish,
how I wish you were here.
We're just
73
Am
G
two lost souls swim-ming in a fish bowl,
year af - ter year,
77
D
C
mf
run - ning o - ver the same old ground.
What have we found?
80
Am
The same old
fears.
Wish you were here.
83
G
rit.
mp

Alfred